Henri Chaumont

A Priest Living the Spirit of Jesus in the Heart of the World

DANIEL MOULINET
Priest of St. Francis de Sales

St. Francis
de Sales
Association

CONTENTS

Acknowledgments & Photos

I   Formative Years 1836-1863   1

II   Spreading the Gospel among the People 1864–1868   20

III   Assistant at Sainte Clotilde in Troubled Times 1868–1874   41

IV   Msgr. de Ségur and His Influence   67

V   First Attempts to Start a Salesian Society for Women   84

VI   Daughters and Sons of St. Francis de Sales   100

VII   The Priests of St. Francis de Sales   160

VIII   Father Chaumont—His Ministry   197

Conclusion, Contacts, Bibliography & Photos   230

FOREWORD

This book has been translated into English by Suzanne Gasster-Carrière with the authorization of Fr. Daniel Moulinet, the author of the original French work: *"Au Coeur du monde, Henri Chaumont, un prêtre dans l'Esprit de Jésus."* Some details directly concerned with the Church in Paris have been purposely omitted with the agreement of the author, because they are not of much interest to readers from other countries.

We thank Suzanne Gasster-Carrière for her translation, produced with wholehearted and gracious dedication. We also thank Kathleen Griesemer, who has taken the time to re-read and edit this translation.

May Fr. Chaumont, so well depicted by Fr. Daniel Moulinet, inspire and do much good for all the English readers of his life.

Fr. Daniel MOULINET

Maison Louis Richard
9, Place abbe Larue
69005, LYON, FRANCE

St. François de Sales Society
57-59 rue Leon Frot
75011, PARIS,
FRANCE

Purpose: Ceding rights of the author

I, the undersigned, Daniel Moulinet, author of the book *Au coeur du monde, Henri Chaumont, un pretre dans l'Esprit de Jesus* (*Henri Chaumont, A Priest Living the Spirit of Jesus in the Heart of the World*), give my rights as an author to the St. Francis de Sales Society (Priests, Daughters, Sons of St. Francis de Sales and Salesian Missionaries of Mary Immaculate).

This permission gives them full liberty to edit, distribute, and translate this book as necessary.

The Society will provide me, free of charge, with 30 copies of the published work as well as an example of each of the eventual translations in foreign languages.

Given for the value of this right,

Paris, June 11, 2010

(Signed)

Fr. Daniel Moulinet

INTRODUCTION

Pope Benedict XVI decided to make the year 2009–2010 the 150th anniversary of the death of the Curé of Ars, a "year of the priesthood." Saint Jean-Marie Vianney is presented as the patron saint of all priests in the world, yet to propose a nineteenth-century figure as a "model" for priests today is not an obvious choice.

Much has changed: perceptions, contemporary society, and an evolution within the Church herself. Thus, we must look at the spirituality of the saint rather than at the conditions of his life in order to understand this choice. And yet the two are inseparable. Spirituality is formed, developed, and tested in the events of daily life. We can only approach an understanding by taking the time to examine the life of the man who conceived and lived it.

The same is true of Fr. Henri Chaumont (1838–1896). He, too, is a man of the nineteenth century, the founder of an association of priests, the Society of Priests of St. Francis de Sales, and of groups of laypeople, the Daughters and the Sons of St. Francis de Sales. Fr. Chaumont's Catechist Missionaries, formed from among the Daughters of St. Francis de Sales, is today a congregation of religious women, the Salesian Missionaries of Mary Immaculate. They have carried the Gospel to the farthest corners of the world. All of these groups are thriving today. They trace their spirituality back to Francis de Sales, but they do not forget that it is thanks to Fr. Chaumont that they do so.

Like Jean-Marie Vianney, who after a brief period as assistant pastor remained until the end of his life in a small village even though he was renowned throughout the world, Henri Chaumont did not become famous through a brilliant priestly career. His ministry was relatively short; he died at the age of fifty-eight working only in Paris in rather secondary positions. He was neither pastor of a parish nor a member of the diocesan administration; nor for that matter, was he one of the gifted preachers who brought fame to the pulpit of Paris' Notre Dame cathedral. Yet his work has borne fruit worldwide.

Many of our contemporaries see the encouragement of the participation of the laity in the Catholic Church as a recent phenomenon; however, the example of Fr. Chaumont, following the teachings of St. Francis de Sales, demonstrates that such an apostolate began to develop in the middle of the nineteenth century, especially for Christian women. In this area Fr. Chaumont was certainly a pioneer.

This awakening of the laity was by no means the work of a single individual. Having taken his inspiration from the spirituality of Francis de Sales, Fr. Chaumont was guided in turn by his "spiritual father," Msgr. Gaston de Ségur, to encourage

Christian women in their spiritual journey. The work of these Christian women in nineteenth-century France is well known. Fr. Chaumont was able to take advantage of his appointment as assistant at Sainte Clotilde, in one of the wealthiest parts of Paris, to develop his particular charisma and encourage the women of his parish to combine spiritual progress and missionary work in the world. Among his parishioners he found an extraordinary person, Mme Carré de Malberg, and with her he founded the Daughters of St. Francis de Sales.

In 1919 Msgr. August Laveille[1] published an important biography of Fr. Chaumont; two years previously he had written about the life of Mme Carré de Malberg. After Fr. Chaumont's death and 11 years after Msgr. Laveille's biography was published, Msgr. Debout, director of the Society of Priests of Francis de Sales,[2] revisited the details of the life of Henri Chaumont in preparation for the hearings commenced to initiate Fr. Chaumont's cause for canonization in the Archdiocese of Paris.

---

[1] Msgr. August Laveille (1856–1928) authored several studies on the history of Catholic teaching and several biographies.

[2] While he was vicar of Montreuil-sur-Mer, Fr. Henri Debout (1857–1936) encountered the Society of the Priests of St. Francis de Sales. He was secretary to Fr. Chaumont for a year, later became General Director of the Priests (1922), and worked for Fr. Chaumont's canonization.

Msgr. Debout, one of the important voices in this process, also authored a biography of Fr. Chaumont, focusing on the Society of Priests of St. Francis de Sales. This new study did not detract from the importance of the preceding work by Msgr. Laveille. In the process of canonization, the majority of witnesses (thirty-four out of fifty-five), said that they found a faithful portrait of their founder in Msgr. Laveille's book.

Ninety years later it seems important to look again at this portrait in order to do justice to Fr. Chaumont for his role in the societies he founded, and also with an eye to the inspiration that his life and insights may give to all diocesan priests. The work that follows hopes to be only a step toward a fuller knowledge of this founding father whose writings should be explored in their entirety.[3]

---

[3] Henri Chaumont's papers are conserved in the archives of the Salesian Centre (57-59 rue Leon Frot, 75011, Paris, France). They include documentation of the Daughters of St. Francis de Sales, the instructions Fr. Chaumont addressed to Christian Women, eight notebooks of sermons, and 64 notebooks of letters by Fr. Chaumont.

Fr. Chaumont's confessional

Caroline Carré de Malberg

The chapel at Venerable Caroline Carré de
Malberg's home where her body is buried.

CHAPTER I

FORMATIVE YEARS (1836–1863)

The first years of the life of Henri Chaumont are not well documented. Even though we can follow the events of his youth and his intellectual formation, we have no information about the development of his spiritual life. Nevertheless, some important reference points are known: his meeting and relationship with Msgr. de Ségur, his discovery of the thought of St. Francis de Sales, and his ordination to the priesthood.

The First Years

Henri Chaumont was born in Paris on December 11, 1838, on rue du Four, between the church of Saint Sulpice and the "Latin Quarter."

He was the second son of Pierre Chaumont and Ann Korsten, a family of staunch Catholics. The father, a furniture maker, was born in Franche-Compté, a region of deeply rooted religious traditions that produced many vocations for the Church. It was even able to supply priests to other areas of the country that recovered more slowly from the religious persecutions during the French Revolution. Pierre Chaumont, like so many others, came to Paris looking for work.

There he married Ann Korsten, the daughter of a tailor living on boulevard Montparnasse. In order to care for his family, Pierre set himself up as a wine merchant.

The couple had eight children. Paul, the eldest, became a shopkeeper; then came Henri and Marie, followed by Ernest, who became a church musician. The others included Abel; Marthe (who became a Daughter of Francis de Sales and died in Périgueux in 1917); Madeline, who married a successful tailor in Paris; and Joseph, who died in early childhood.

Henri was baptized in the church of Saint-Germain-des-Prés when he was five days old.[4] When he was five years old, his mother consecrated him to the Virgin Mary, in the chapel of the Jesuit residence on rue de Sèvres. His parents took special care to encourage his Christian and humane qualities, already apparent at a young age: "his precocious intelligence, … his vitality, his good humor and playfulness, … his early indications of piety, … and his integrity." (Msgr. Laveille)

Even at the age of five or six, he declared that he wanted to be a priest. He listened, enthralled, to the letters written by missionaries and read to him by his parents from the *Annals of the Propagation of the Faith* and *Holy Childhood*, and announced that he wanted to be a missionary to convert the Chinese.

---

[4] His godfather, who was also his uncle, Louis Chaumont, lived in the same building as his parents; his godmother was his aunt, Jeanne Justine Horsten.

When he was eight, his parents sent him and his older brother Paul to Louveciennes, to a small boarding school that had been recommended to his parents. The country air was perhaps good for the children, but Henri was unhappy far from his family.

First Communion and a Spiritual Crisis

1848 was a time of upheaval in Paris. On February 22, a first revolution overthrew the king, Louis Philippe, and sent him into exile. The Republic was proclaimed. For the first time, an Assembly was elected by universal (male) suffrage. The atmosphere was extremely tense. The announcement of the closing of the National Work Shops, which gave work to the unemployed, provoked a new uprising. The Archbishop of Paris, Msgr. Affre, was killed when he attempted to intervene. Maintaining order became the priority; the presidential regime put in place at the end of the year opened the door for an authoritarian government after the coup d'état of December 1851. A year later, Louis-Napoléon declared the Second Empire, taking the name of Napoléon III.

The events of 1848 caused Henri Chaumont's parents to bring the two children back home. They placed Henri to board half time in M Dugard's school, recently opened on the rue du Four. The child prepared for his first Communion in the parish of Saint Sulpice, which enjoyed an excellent reputation in Paris. He made his first Communion on the 21st of June 1850, before his twelfth birthday.[5] On that day the priest who was Henri's catechist introduced him to Fr. de Ségur, whose influence would be a determining factor in his life.

In spite of these promising beginnings, the child experienced a spiritual crisis. At his own request, his parents took him to hear a preacher at Notre Dame des Victoires. This priest was probably addressing an audience imbued with superficial piety. He told his listeners that most of their confessions were invalid, being made without sufficient preparation and serious contrition. The child was infected with the sickness of scrupulosity, fearing that such was his case. He made confession after confession, never satisfied with his sincerity or his absolution. He changed confessors frequently. In spite of all, he maintained his desire to become a priest, but his confessors would not take him seriously when they became aware of his spiritual disposition.

His father sent him to be apprenticed to a clock-maker, M Joly, on the rue de Sèvres, who offered him a

---

[5] The child's age when he made his first Communion is not surprising. Having first Holy Communion and Confirmation at the same time was established by the liturgical reform of Pope Pius X (published August 6, 1910). Until then children received their first Communion at different ages: for boys it was sometimes put off until the age of fifteen. In this context Henri Chaumont's Communion was perhaps a little early, but he was recognized as especially pious and studious at catechism.

4

contract for four years. Although the young man had a solid professional conscience, he nevertheless continued to be haunted by his religious scruples, to the point that it weakened his health. Fr. de Ségur maintained his contact with him. At the time, Fr. de Ségur was leaving for Rome to be an auditor at the tribunal of Rote. He recommended Henri to one of his friends, an assistant at Saint Sulpice, Fr. Bayle,[6] who finally was able to calm this two-year-long crisis of faith. Nevertheless, it left its marks on the young man.

"The Servant of God maintained a moral punctiliousness. His severity toward himself and the rigid standards to which he held his disciples especially regarding holy virtue, show it."[7]

The Minor Seminaries of Versailles and Montmorillon

When his contract with the clock-maker ended, Henri Chaumont was able to return to his intellectual formation for the priesthood. He spent several months at Louveciennes to refresh his scholarly preparation. In the spring of 1855, he entered the fourth year at the minor seminary in Versailles, recommended by Fr. de Ségur, who had recently returned from Rome. This seminary is austere and its chapel maintains the

---

[6] Fr. Charles Bayle (1839–1873) was to become vicar general of Paris.

[7] Testimony is by Fr. Debout, from the *Summarium* in the process of beatification of Fr. Chaumont.

memory of a miraculous healing that had taken place ten years earlier: a blind student was healed at the moment he received Holy Communion.

Henri was true to the sense of his vocation. His parents were concerned about their son Paul, who had left home and was involved with friends who had a bad influence on him. Henri offered himself "as a ransom"[8] for his brother every day. Nevertheless, his professors were not fully convinced; they interpreted the boy's homesickness as a lack of energy. Finding his accomplishments mediocre, they held him back at the beginning of the next school year. However, Henri's teacher in the next class, Fr. Muret, was demanding as well as highly cultivated, and under his tutelage the young man learned to enjoy study. He wrote to his parents:

I am desperate. I work all day; I fall asleep reviewing what I studied. I don't even allow myself to write letters, or to participate in recess, and yet I look as if I were lazy, compared to my teacher! What a model. He doesn't sleep, he doesn't eat, he works ten times as much as I do, and yet his good health is astonishing.[9]

---

[8]In a letter to his parents, cited by Msgr. Debout, "Le Chanoine Henri Chaumont and the Sanctification of a Priest," 1930. He practiced a devotion of the time usually made to the Sacred Heart. One offered reparation to the Lord in place of a sinner who would not ask forgiveness for his sins.

[9] In an unpublished letter to his parents, 1856, quoted by Msgr. Laveille.

Living so rigorously, Henri indeed made progress, and at the end of the year was graded eighth out of twenty-one students. But his health was weakened and conditions at the school were not propitious. Fr. de Ségur suggested to his parents that Henri finish his first formation for the priesthood at the minor seminary of Montmorillon. The priest was on friendly terms with the bishop of Poitiers, Msgr. Pie. He was confident of the level of preparation in this school, and especially of their teaching of spirituality. He sent several young men who seemed especially promising to study at Montmorillon and even paid for part of their schooling. After 1857, he himself sometimes went there to lead retreats. At the time, the school was located in a pleasant setting. In front of the seventeenth-century buildings, a broad terrace overlooked the panorama of the Guartempe valley.

Many minor seminaries were then "mixed," that is offering preparation for both civil and ecclesiastical careers (they also welcomed the sons of well-to-do families wanting the advantage of quality education in a respectable setting). Msgr. Pie's was a "pure seminary" oriented only toward the preparation of priests. Every year he conferred the tonsure on third-year students, and the upper classes had to begin wearing ecclesiastical clothing. Théophile Vénard is one of the students who graduated from this seminary. He became a missionary in Tonkin, where he was martyred in 1861. He was beatified in 1909.

Henri Chaumont arrived at Montmorillon in the fall of 1858. At the request of Msgr. de Ségur, he was admitted directly to classes in philosophy, an indication of the good opinion that the faculty had of his intellectual level and an acknowledgment of his intense work at the minor seminary in Versailles. The young man especially appreciated his professor of philosophy, Fr. Charbonneau, who taught him the importance of a demanding search for truth. At the end of the school year, Henri was ranked fifth among thirty-five students. He formed lasting friendships with some of his fellow students, for example, Fr. Bougoin, the future bishop of Périgueux, and Fr. Périvier, who would become vicar general of the diocese of Poitiers. In addition to his studies, Henri was given the responsibility of monitoring a dormitory of about thirty students. He demonstrated the ability both to exercise authority and to be affectionate toward his charges. On several occasions his comrades noticed his attempts at mortification and his practices of special piety even though he tried to keep them secret. He loved to pray in front of the Blessed Sacrament that was displayed in an octagonal chapel in the courtyard of the school, formerly the tomb of the lords of Montmorillon.

Having received the tonsure from Msgr. Pie on April 4, 1859, Henri Chaumont was admitted to his second year of philosophy at the seminary of Issy-les-Moulineaux, once again on the recommend-ation of

Msgr. de Ségur. The priests of Saint Sulpice directed this school founded in 1641.

Seminary of Saint Sulpice

When Henri Chaumont began his studies at Saint Sulpice, the current buildings had not yet been constructed:

At Issy, the rooms are small and austere; there is a watercolor made in 1892 that shows walls cracked and patches of peeling paint. A low window opens out over the roofs. There is an iron frame bed, a study table over which hangs a crucifix, a tiny table holding the washbasin, a trunk, and a bookshelf.[10]

Henri Chaumont chose Fr. Pinault as his confessor, an old man with an austere appearance. Due to his age and bad health, Fr. Pinault was often not available; a further difficulty in the young man's spiritual life was that he could see Msgr. de Ségur only once or twice a year, during vacations.

Among his fellow students, several were to become well known: first of all, Maurice d'Hulst with whom he maintained a lasting friendship and who has a place further on in this biography. Despite the difference in social class, the spiritual paternity of Msgr. de Ségur was a bond between them. Henri's other early friends

---

[10] Marthe de Hédouville, *Msgr. de Ségur, Sa vie, son action, (1820–1881), 1957.*

9

were to become priests in Paris, vicars general or bishops. De Bretenières, who became a priest with the Foreign Missions, was martyred in Korea in 1866.

Fr. Courtade devoted himself to evangelizing in Paris along with Fr. d'Hulst. Henri Chaumont tells us about daily life at Saint Sulpice:

5:00 a.m., the exitateur, who rose at 4:00 a.m., half opens the door of each cell, announcing to the sleepers, "Benedicamus Domino." If they do not respond with "Deo gratias," to prove that they are awake, they will hear the greeting a second and even a third time. They wash and dress quickly, straighten their cells, carry water to fill the buckets in their rooms, all in twenty-five minutes.

At 5:30 the bell calls all of us to prayer. The quickest and the most pious are already in the chapel, adoring the Blessed Sacrament. Everyone is present in the hall for devotions; the director has taken care to light the lamp. A bench that goes all around the room is the only furniture, and only the sick have permission to use it. The others pray a half hour on their knees and the second thirty minutes standing up. At 6:00 the seminarians, wearing the surplice, attend Mass; most of them receive Communion. From 7:00 to 8:00, they remain in their cells where, as Saint-Beuve remarked, they are only answerable to their conscience. From there they go to the refectory for the piece of dry bread, which constitutes their breakfast. At 9:30 class, at

10:30 back to their cells till 11:45, the time when everyone, on their knees and bare-headed, examines his conscience.[11]

At noon, directors and students are together in the refectory seated around the same tables. In front of each place, there is a half-liter of wine, bread, and on each plate, an abundant serving of food. The meal is eaten in silence while the rule is read aloud.

The seminarians go from the table to the chapel, where they recite the Angelus, and then silence is broken for the first time in the day. During recess no one is allowed to remain alone. All must join the first comrade they encounter and walk in groups.

At the end of recreation, the bell ringing imposes silence again. The students take polite leave of one another and go to the chapel to honor Our Lady, as they recite the rosary. They return to their cells until the next class, from 3:30 to 4:30, followed by a little free time and then individual work until the father superior leads the hour of spiritual reading. At 7:00 supper, a recess, and then prayer. Bedtime was at 9:00. (Marthe de Hédouville)

It is easy to see from this description how the whole process of formation at Saint Sulpice favored spiritual over intellectual growth and encouraged an inward

---

[11] This is a private reflection, examining the actions of the morning.

piety by the scarcity of social interaction among the seminarians. It was in this first year of study that Henri Chaumont became acquainted with the thought of St. Francis de Sales.

I had my first revelation of devotion for Francis de Sales at Issy. Until then, even though I was the spiritual child of Msgr. de Ségur, who was fully devoted to Francis de Sales, I had not really felt attracted to this spirituality. At Montmorillon I didn't think about it at all. If someone had asked me at that time what saint I preferred I would have said that I liked the character of Saint Francis, nothing more.

Grace was waiting for me at Issy. It was during my first lunch at the seminary at Issy, along with the sound of forks on plates, after the reading of Holy Scripture, that I heard the call of the good Lord. Someone was reading the Letters of Francis de Sales. For me, it was a revelation, a light, a moment of grace to last forever. I went that very day to see the bursar who had been named to be my director, I told him that I had been so impressed by the reading of the letters of Saint Francis de Sales that I wanted to ask him if he had some of the works of the saint so that I could start a personal study. I immediately chose the Letters, since it was that reading that had touched me so deeply. He gave me a volume and from that day on I never abandoned my study of Francis de Sales.

I kept it up at the same time as I was reading philosophy; I carried the beloved volume with me everywhere. That was my point of departure, the voice of grace. Our Lord speaks when he wills it; but he doesn't always speak that clearly.[12]

After a year at Issy, Henri Chaumont was admitted to the theological seminary at Saint Sulpice in Paris (October 1, 1860). The superior was Fr. Carrière, a specialist in canon law, and superior general of the Company of Saint Sulpice; Fr. Carbon, his assistant, was the "director of the seminary"; Fr. Icard taught canon law; and Fr. Le Hir, Scripture, along with Fr. Grandvaux, who was much sought after as a spiritual director.[13] He agreed to guide the young man's studies, perhaps at the request of Msgr. de Ségur,[14] and he remained afterward Henri's counselor. After hearing the life of Francis de Sales in the refectory, Henri undertook an analysis of *The Introduction to the Devout Life*. He began to outline *The Spiritual Direction of Saint Francis de Sales*, organizing the

---

[12] Unpublished letter quoted by Msgr. Laveille.

[13] Charles August Grandvaux (1819–1885), a priest at Saint Sulpice in 1847, taught moral theology and Scripture. His obituary especially emphasized his kind heart. The ties of friendship and confidence between Msgr. Grandvaux and Fr. Chaumont lasted for a long time: Fr. Emmanuel de la Perche testified that it was Fr. Grandvaux, his spiritual director, who advised Henri Chaumont in 1876 to go to meet the founder of the order. *Summarium*, p. 88.

[14] We know that Msgr. de Ségur did as much for another of his spiritual sons, Maurice d'Hulst.

teachings of the saint concerning each virtue. During the hearings of the Ordinary concerning the beatification of Henri Chaumont, Msgr. Debout also spoke of the appreciation of two companions of the future saint from his time at the seminary:

Fr. Pousset told me that Henri Chaumont was not among the brightest of his class, but still, above average. (Seventh of ten.) It was rather his unrelenting study that gained him the admiration of his comrades, and his company was sought out among the students. I'm not sure which of the witnesses to Henri's years at Saint Sulpice said that his whole being radiated authority and severity, making him appear too harsh. Nevertheless, he was unfailingly kind, a character trait that overshadowed his severity. (Summarium)

Preparation for Ordination

Henri Chaumont continued toward his ordination, through the usual process, receiving minor[15] orders (December 21, 1861), sub-deacon (June 14, 1862), and deacon (December 20, 1862). From that time on, he received the honor of participating in the direction of catechumens in the diocese of Saint Sulpice along with a few other seminarians. They worked with 250 children of the best Parisian families. Henri's

---

[15] Minor orders are porter, lector, exorcist, and acolyte. Sub-deacon was earlier considered a minor order but became a major order at the end of the twelfth century, making it the entry into the clergy.

particular responsibility was to prepare young girls for their first Communion, under the direction of Fr. Guillot, in collaboration with Frs. d'Hulst and de Cabanoux.[16] He already served as spiritual counselor for his younger sisters, Madeline and Marthe. The latter was in school at Evry, Grandbourg, near Paris, with the sisters of Notre Dame-de-Sion. Her sister, Madeline, gave testimony to his influence on her life:

I myself studied catechism with Henri at Saint Sulpice. This Servant of God, while his role was to teach us, touched us with his kindness, and his lively mind held our attention.

For the feast days, he organized the little plays that were at that time usual in catechism classes at Saint Sulpice. When I was preparing for my first Holy Communion, I was in school with the sisters of Notre Dame de Sion. My brother, who was still a seminarian, wrote me such beautiful letters that the mother superior read them to the whole community.[17]

As Henri was preparing himself for priestly ordination, he had doubts about his ability to offer the Sacrament of Reconciliation.

---

[16] Fr. Thomas Joly de Cabanoux (1840–1925) would be pastor of Notre Dame des Champs and then of St. Thomas Aquinas, both parishes in Paris.
[17] *Summarium.*

He consulted his spiritual director. With several other seminarians he founded an association whose official name, The Association of Saint Sulpice, quickly became The White Oak Society. Its members proposed, once their preparation for priesthood was complete, to live in great simplicity. Their rule:

The members of the Association have resolved to shun not only what could be considered secular luxury or could become the occasion for wanting it, but also, within the limits of decency and cleanliness, to maintain rigorous ecclesiastical simplicity. They will have only furniture made from white oak, beech, walnut, or similar woods of humble significance.[18]

The seminarians were conscious of the difference in incomes among the Paris clergy, which tempted some "high-ranking priests" to lead a life that separated them from the majority of their flock. On the other hand, they were also conscious of their mission in this milieu, and following the example of Msgr. de Ségur, resolved not to be "career oriented" or at least to maintain a life of simplicity whatever their future position in the Church. Msgr. de Ségur himself went to the seminary for the last meeting of the White Oak Society before the members received their first assignments. In his speech to them, delivered in the

---

[18] Association of Saint Sulpice, *Rule.*

cell of Fr. Grandvaux, he encouraged them to persevere in these dispositions.[19]

Henri Chaumont's ordination was interrupted by an unfortunate incident. On December 19, 1863, in the church of Saint Sulpice, thirty-five deacons from Saint Sulpice and from the seminary of Foreign Missions were to be ordained by Bishop Darboy; and at the same time, he was to confer minor orders on men from other seminaries. The ceremony had begun and several of the rites carried out when the archbishop fainted, as a result of a prolonged fast. He was carried to the sacristy for care, but did not regain consciousness for some time. Since he was obliged to break his fast, he said that he could not continue the ceremony.

Opinions were divided as to what the correct response should be: Some believed that since the laying on of hands had taken place, part of the ritual should not be repeated; others were convinced that all should be begun over again. Finally there was a consultation with the Holy See. As a result, the archbishop delegated Msgr. Maret, bishop *in partibus* of Sura, and

---

[19] The regime established by the French Concordat (in place until 1905) created a rigid hierarchy among the clergy. Their incomes were linked to the functions they carried out: vicars general, canons, first- and second-class priests, assistant priests, vicars. At the bottom of the scale were the "prêtres habitués" who had no official function and whose only income was the honoraria of Masses, whatever their brothers in the hierarchy saw fit to give them.

dean of the faculty of theology at the Sorbonne, to carry out the ordination on January 18, 1864. The intimate ceremony took place in the chapel of the seminary of Saint Sulpice. Henri Chaumont celebrated his first Mass the next day, in the chapel of Saint François Xavier at Saint Sulpice, where a few years earlier he had studied the catechism of perseverance.[20] On the eve of this Mass, he wrote to his parents:

I have desired this great day and I continue to desire it because I am seeking only the glory of God and the salvation of souls. If you ask me what my feelings are at this moment, I have to say that I don't know which is stronger, thankfulness to our Lord or the sense of my own unworthiness. These mingled feelings aren't upsetting, but . . . but . . . how should I say it? All of it is a mystery. There is no common measure between what God's plan for me may be and what I am; I can only remain silent, because no possible words of humility could express the infinite unworthiness that I feel.

So, dear parents, I can only turn to God. He called me and brought me this far. He wants me to climb the last step to the altar. Since he wishes it, here I am. I throw myself head first into the ocean of his mercy. If it is his will, I will go this last distance and stand at the altar. I will command him to come into my hands. I will sit

---

[20] The term refers to an extended catechism, more detailed and voluntary, that follows first Communion.

at his place and say, "Yes, I forgive you," and at the same time, he will forgive. Yes, I will do all of this. I will have the right and the consolation to be able to say, "My Lord, if I dare to do all of this, it is because you yourself have ordered it."

Do you understand, my dear parents, this combined sense of gratitude and humility? All my fears and all my hopes, sadness, and joy, but most of all, as God's mercy is infinitely greater than our wretchedness, it is one of the most beautiful signs of his infinite power to seek out among the lowliest those he wishes to raise up. I rejoice that I have been chosen. I rejoice, not for myself, nor ultimately because there are souls to be saved, but because of Him; by my elevation, he brings about the saving of these dear souls and the glorification of his goodness.[21]

---

[21] A letter to his parents, December 17, 1863, quoted by Msgr. Debout.

CHAPTER II

SPREADING THE GOSPEL
AMONG THE PEOPLE (1864–1868)

Father Chaumont was assigned to work in a very poor area of Paris. The young Fr. Chaumont found that he was led to take pastoral initiatives that awakened his missionary spirit. Msgr. de Ségur guided him unerringly in this area, watching over the unfolding of Henri's priestly talents, and showing confidence in his abilities to be a spiritual director.

The Parish of Saint Marcel

Fr. Chaumont's first assignment was as an assistant in the parish of Saint Marcel, which had been created a few years earlier to serve a new area of Paris. Victor Hugo gave a realistic and poetic description of the surroundings:

The ground is pebbly, covered with trampled grass, . . . the rickety mill turns in the wind, the wheels extracting rock from the quarries, and there are dance halls and bars at the corners of the cemetery. There is the mysterious charm about the looming walls, whose shadow cuts across the empty fields filled with sunlight and butterflies.

Anyone who has wandered like us, through these lonely spaces . . . perhaps we could call them the limbo of Paris, will have caught sight, here and there, in the most desolate spot, at an unexpected moment, behind a scrawny hedge or in the angle of a melancholy wall, of children, in tumultuous groups, pale, muddy, dusty, ragged, disheveled, crowned with cornflowers playing pigoche.[22] These are little refugees from poor families. The outer boulevard is their source of fresh air; the outskirts of the city belong to them.[23]

Evangelization of this area began in 1847 with the creation of two parishes at the southern end of Boulevard de l'Hôpital: Notre Dame de la Gare and Saint Marcel de la Maison Blanche, on avenue d'Italie. The opening of the Avenue des Gobelins and the Boulevard Saint Marcel brought a new population, and Bishop Sibour, sensitive to the well-being of the poor in his diocese, requested the creation of a new parish, Saint Marcel de la Salpêtrière. It was centered on the Boulevard de l'Hôpital, continuing from Place d'Italie to the Austerlitz Train Station. Its territory was practically untouched. The first pastor was Fr. Pierre-Nicolas Morisot (1808–1874), who built the first church, a very simple structure:[24]

---

[22] It is a children's game resembling hopscotch, consisting of shooting a coin out of a circle traced in the ground, by throwing another coin onto it, or of making a coin jump as far as possible by hitting its edges.

[23] Victor Hugo, *Les Miserables*, Part III.

[24] This was replaced by a modern building in 1962.

He was a priest of mature years, with a solemn demeanor. . . . Perfectly courteous . . . , kindly, calm, distinguished, clever at business, the perfect example of the priest-administrator so commonly found in Paris. (Msgr. Laveille)

Along with Fr. Chaumont, three other priests worked with Fr. Morisot: the aged Fr. Evrard, "prêtre habitué"; Fr. Léger, the second assistant, "a studious man, dependable and punctual in carrying out his responsibilities in the parish, who devoted his free time to learning oriental languages," (quotes by Msgr. Laveille); and Fr. Varnet, the first assistant, were fully devoted to the ministry of bringing the Gospel to the poor of the area.

The Sisters of Charity had begun their own work of evangelization even before the founding of the parish of Saint Marcel. Since 1833 Sister Rosalie Rendu was known and appreciated for her work inspired by Frédéric Ozanam and his companions, who were a prelude to the Society of Saint Vincent de Paul. At the time of Henri Chaumont's arrival, Sister Rosalie was present for a conference concerning the area, motivated by the founding of a free school for boys. The Sisters of Charity directed a school for girls and a boarding school for girls from well-off families, run by two sisters, the Mlles de La Motte.

The number of practicing Catholics was low. The *pascalisants* were probably not more than 5 percent,[25] overwhelmingly women.

Evangelizing the People

Henri Chaumont had many responsibilities in his new ministry: first of all, the usual tasks of an assistant. Since he was the newest member of the clerical staff, he was called to celebrate the earliest Sunday Mass, at 6:00 a.m., the Mass attended by workers and domestic servants. It was the time to direct simple exhortations to an unsophisticated community, whereas the homily at the High Mass was an exercise in oratory. At the beginning, like many young priests, Henri took Bourdaloue as a model[26] and spoke about difficult points of doctrine, the nature of faith, and its elements and conditions.

That was not the way to reach the people who were entrusted to his ministry. Fr. Chaumont found that he was nearly the only person to pray in front of the Blessed Sacrament. So, in 1865, he began the practice of Perpetual Adoration in the parish. It became widespread in Paris in the second half of the nineteenth

---

[25] The term refers to Catholics who were satisfied with only fulfilling their "Easter duty." (Note: The term comes from the French word "Pâques"—Easter.)

[26] Louis Bourdaloue (1632–1704) enjoyed a wide reputation as preacher at the (French) Court. Many editions of his sermons were published, beginning in 1707.

century. He addressed himself at first to a few practicing Catholics before he could reach a broader spectrum of his flock.

Fr. Chaumont also encouraged frequent Communion, overcoming the resistance due perhaps to the lingering influence of Jansenism.[27] The sense of a missionary vocation, gained in his childhood from reading *Annals of the Propagation of the Faith and Holy Childhood,* remained with him. He asked his associates in the Society of Perpetual Adoration for a "crusade of prayer" in favor of women who had not learned about Christianity. Later, this initiative would take another form.

The young priest was greatly appreciated as a confessor. His guiding principle was St. Francis de Sales, who countered the rigor inherited from Jansenism, and encouraged the confessor to accompany the penitent as she or he attempted to make amends for past failings. Msgr. de Ségur entrusted some of his penitents to him, which introduced Fr. Chaumont to a broader circle of the faithful. As a mark of his faith in the young priest, Msgr. de Ségur asked him to hear the confessions of his own mother. His

---

[27] According to Msgr. Laveille, this practice began with the teaching in a normal school founded in this area at the beginning of the eighteenth century. The teachers, who attended Mass regularly and brought their students, rarely received Communion.

personal schedule shows how available he made himself in the parish:

Fr. Chaumont, assistant at Saint Marcel, hears Confessions:

1. *Every day at 5:30 in the morning.*[28]
2. *Every day at 6:30, except Wednesday.*
3. *Thursdays at 8:30 in the morning and at 8:00 in the evening.*
4. *Tuesday, Saturday, and Sunday all day except during Masses. Inquire at the sacristy.*
5. *Confession for the sick in their home.*
6. *Confession for the handicapped in the chapel of Saint Joseph.*
7. *Confession for gentlemen: Tuesday and Friday 8:30 in the evening Boulevard de l'Hôpital.*[29]

His nephew, Fr. Paul Chaumont, commented:

He was an excellent spiritual director, firm, clear, perceptive, the supernatural seemed to combine with extraordinary natural gifts. He was very busy and gave the impression that he was in fact very busy, but ready to take the time to deal with things that were worthwhile.[30]

---

[28] After hearing confessions, he celebrated the 6:00 a.m. Mass.

[29] It is worth noting that confessions for men were held in the school rather than at the church, perhaps a more neutral place, where they would not be seen going to confession.

[30] Quoted by Msgr. Debout. It is probable that he was in fact referring to the priest in later years.

Msgr. Laveille reported that the dispersion of its members and their different functions brought about the gradual disappearance of The White Oak Society. Nevertheless, Henri Chaumont remained faithful to its spirit. At the request of his former White Oak companions he composed a new version of the *Rule* recognizable in spirit with the ideals they had formulated: modesty in appearance, wearing the cassock, a simple way of life, sobriety,[31] and respect for the opinions of others.

The young assistant did not shut himself up in his church. To evangelize among the people, he had several natural gifts that he knew how to use well:

He possessed the exterior gifts of a popular evangelizer to a high degree: he was small but well formed, his expression was open, he had a broad forehead, a welcoming smile, where you could sometimes catch a note of mischievousness; along with this appearance, he had a gift for conversation, his language was imaged, lively, and engaging; his tone of voice varied, moving easily from gentle irony to deep emotion. (Msgr. Laveille)

In order to reach his flock of working people, he participated in activities that the religious sisters had already begun: recreational events, after which religious objects were given as prizes. He was struck by the reaction of a rag-seller who came to see him

---

[31] This rule was particularly emphasized.

holding in his hand a volume of *A Brief Explanation of Christian Doctrine,* which he had received as a prize in one of these sports the night before. He said that he had spent the night reading it and came, in tears, to thank the young assistant pastor for this revelation of the truth that he had never understood before. In this spirit, Fr. Chaumont began a series of meetings aimed at this audience.

How could he draw to the Church these crowds of ragged workers, irreverent and light-hearted, easily stirred up by agents of secret societies that turned them against priests and Christian doctrine? He had to start by meeting them in a simple setting rather than a church. To explain his message, he would have to present himself as a "preacher in a short coat."[32]

Fr. Chaumont took charge of everything. To the right of the church of Saint Marcel, there was a big rectangular building that was used several times a week for the children's catechism, but it was free Monday evenings. The young priest decided to call together a group of rag-sellers, asking their wives to convince them to attend. He had to begin with a talk by a layperson, adapted to the level and tastes of his audience. Then he would give a talk on a religious topic, and in between, all would sing some popular religious songs accompanied by the harmonium (a musical instrument) *used for catechism classes.*

---

[32]This expression reminds us that priests then wore the cassock in everyday life.

The plan was easily put into place. Henri Chaumont's father was an effective speaker; his talks, filled with his own faith, had already brought some to the Church. He agreed to present the opening talks alternatively with a former magistrate, M Gautier, who walked for miles through the area, bringing a kind word to its unfortunate residents. The priest's younger brother, Ernest, who was a talented musician, led the music with the harmonium. Pastor Morizot [sic] gave his consent for the project to begin.

Carefully chosen, discreet invitations brought a small group to the events. The speakers pleased the listeners, and Fr. Chaumont's lively talks were a great success, so much so that by Easter the recently formed activity had produced thirty notable conversions. Soon each meeting brought about at least one conversion; in a short time the crowds were too large for the hall![33] *(Msgr. Laveille)*

This kind of popular evangelization, outside of a church building, on secular subjects presented by laypeople and combined with religious instruction by a priest, is quite close to what the Society of St. Francis Xavier had been organizing since the 1840s. It was clear that music and speakers who speak their language, could draw a working-class audience, but they might be put off by the cultural aspect of the evening if it were presented immediately.

---

[33] Msgr. Laveille adds that Fr. Chaumont tried to interest wealthy women in this project, which seems to indicate that besides being educational and evangelizing, it had a charitable purpose.

In this attitude on the part of Fr. Chaumont, there might be a spirit similar to that of St. Francis de Sales, who said, *"You can catch more flies with a teaspoon of honey than with a barrel of vinegar,"* an invitation to act with gentleness.

Thus in the nineteenth century, in what was to become the thirteenth *arrondissement* of Paris, a whole population of rag-sellers was living. At the beginning of the following century, these people were displaced onto the site of the old ramparts, which later became the outer boulevard.[34] Msgr. Laveille wrote about the state of the religious life of the people living in these conditions:

Most of the children are raised without God, without notions of morality, are also deprived of catechism and first Communion.[35] If exceptionally they make a first Communion, it is hastily prepared; no priest takes them into his care afterward and they begin a wretched life that lacks even the light of hope. It is not that they have no respect for religion or refuse Christianity; they observe in their experience that such practices are for the wealthy and the leisure classes and therefore have nothing to do with people like themselves.

---

[34] The Jesuit Pierre Lhande, concerned for these displaced groups of the poor, wrote *Le Christ dans la banlieue, 1927* ("Christ in the Suburbs") asking that churches and meeting halls be built among the housing units to provide catechism and charitable works.

[35] Catechism took place in the school. Therefore, since no secular education was provided for these children, no religious education was available either.

29

One day, Fr. Chaumont met an elderly couple in the street and asked the husband if he practiced a religion.

"Of course, Father. Now we can think about it."

"What? You didn't think about it before?"

"No. There is a time in life to feed your wife and family and when you've taken care of all of that, then it's God's turn."

Such ideas about religious duty are complicated by an incredible ignorance about the precepts of morality. For the poor, the Sacrament of Marriage is superfluous. You go through with it when you can, when some happy circumstance of family or practical motive brings the couple before the priest.

After giving the Nuptial Blessing to a couple of his young protégés, Fr. Chaumont congratulated them in the presence of the witnesses, who all promised to become good Christians. Before he left, the priest spoke again to the newlyweds, "I wish that you will always live happily together."

To which the husband, delighted, replied, "I'm sure we will; the three years that we've been together have been perfect."

Some might have thought that there was no hope to convert people who lived this way. But Fr. Chaumont insisted that even there the Holy Spirit was at work:

People talk about the "Cité D'ore" (Golden City) with fear and contempt because they don't know it. For me it is with joy that I enter it. Our Lord, whom I carry in me and with me, is always well received. No man has ever refused the last sacraments. I have never heard a word directed against religion or its ministers; the people argue, not over my gold but over the copper of my holy medals; my little books, and as they say, my little visit. They are my dear friends, how I love them.[36]

However, Fr. Chaumont's successes among the working people displeased the militants of secret societies[37] who were spreading their message in the same milieu. Taking advantage of a period when the priest fell seriously ill, the opposing forces spread a slanderous rumor, frequent at the time, when a book by Jules Michelet, *Concerning Priests, Women, and the Family,*[38] was widely read.

Members of the Freemason Lodge conspired, knowing that one man's wife went to confession with Fr. Chaumont, and obliged the unfortunate husband to say in public that he had surprised his wife and the priest in conversation in the house. Faced with the husband's anger, the story went, the priest and the wife had tried to hide in the cellar. But the outraged

---

[36] *"A Sermon on Charity by Father Chaumont"* quoted by Msgr. Laveille.

[37] Msgr. Laveille mentions only the Freemasons. But there were other groups as well, the socialists and republican secret societies called the "Marianne." Under the Second Empire the police were very vigilant and all of these groups were obliged to operate in secret.

[38] In this book published in 1845, the historian denounced the hold that priests had on women, through acting as their directors of conscience: he saw interference in the life of the family in this relationship.

husband followed them. The priest's sickness, the story continues, was a result of the beating he received.

While this slander made the rounds of the cafés and hovels of the "Golden City" and even spread to public markets, the victim was helpless on his bed of pain, ignorant of the grotesque tale and completely unable to defend himself. Emboldened by the lack of protest against their malicious story, the Freemasons sent the story to the slander-sheet newspapers in the neighbourhood. They placed it on their pages with absurd and repulsive comments. In a short time the rumor reached the Archbishop. That was the state of affairs when Fr. Chaumont was informed. The Church authorities found out that the police had investigated, but to no avail, and Archbishop Darboy seemed upset by the scandal that was raging.

"This business is distressing," he said to the prosecutor[39] of the ecclesiastical tribunal. "Who is this Fr. Chaumont? Do you know him personally?"

Fortunately, the question was addressed to Fr. Bayle, who had encouraged the vocation of the young priest and had already been protected from a malicious denunciation.

"Yes, Monseigneur," he replied to the archbishop. "I am even pleased to say that he is one of my children[40]

---

[39]That is the prosecutor of the Ecclesiastical tribunal. Had the accusation been justified, an Ecclesiastical court would have also handled the case; this latter court would have pronounced sanctions according to Canon Law.

[40]Fr. Bayle explained that "one of my children" meant he had been spiritual director for Fr. Chaumont.

and that I have the highest esteem for his virtue."
(Msgr. Laveille)

On the advice of Fr. Bayle, Fr. Chaumont went to the workplace of the man who had started the scandal and obliged him, on pain of being accused of defamation, to admit publicly that he had lied. The price of this admission for the wrongdoer was to allow his wife and children to freely exercise their faith.

"My friend, for my part I forgive you. But you are going to recognize in writing and before witnesses that you accused me falsely; then you will grant your wife and children the liberty to practice their religion."[41]

Another story from the same period of time bears testimony to this "dimorphism or the difference in religious practice between men and women in the nineteenth century: it was difficult for men to overcome their fear of being made fun of by their masculine counterparts if they approached the Church.

He never wanted to let the "lambs he had brought back to the fold" wander away again. A Free mason who threatened him in vain with a revolver to keep him from approaching his daughter, who was dangerously ill, caught the disease himself. The vicar came to him, heard his confession, and gave him Holy Communion, and the fellow recovered.

When Fr. Chaumont saw him again, the man declared that the priest was "cruel." "You must show

---

[41]Quoted by Msgr. Laveille. The civil code put in place by Napoleon gave a nearly absolute power over the family to the father.

that your conversion is sincere. Tomorrow the men's society is meeting: you'll be with us." And indeed the former Freemason marched at the head of the procession with a candle in his hand.[42]

The new convert would serve as an example and his attitude might help some of his companions take the next step toward faith. As testimony to the affection that the parishioners, and particularly members of his group called "Christian Doctrine of Saint Marcel," had for Fr. Chaumont, Msgr. Laveille reported something Henri Chaumont's father said during his last days. The former carpenter, who had so many times spoken as a layperson at the parish meetings organized by his son, was seriously ill. The young priest asked his group to begin a novena asking for his healing. He added prayers of thanksgiving for his evangelization and his personal life. However, Mr. Chaumont continued to get worse, and the faithful expected to end their novena with prayers for the dying rather than prayers of thanksgiving for a recovery. Fr. Chaumont continued to have faith and asked for a sign on the last day of the novena, when he would celebrate a Mass and Holy Communion with this intention. Here he saw an opportunity to strengthen the faith of his flock. He asked his father to cooperate in his plan. The old man, whose faith was as great as his son's, accepted.

The very fact that the sick man could be brought to the chapel to attend a Mass celebrated by his son, was already a miracle. This first miracle, whatever God's plan for the future, would be a sign of the power of

---

[42]A story Fr. Chaumont told during a retreat in 1888, quoted by Msgr. Debout.

prayer. And this living sign would be more convincing to the minds of the newly converted than any number of speeches. Without hesitation, Fr. Chaumont asked this favor of God. Then he asked his father to participate in this plan and promised him that he would have assistance from on high. "My God," said the old man, filled with faith, "I only want what you want. You are powerful enough to accomplish this miracle. Let your will, not mine, be done." (Msgr. Laveille)

And in fact, Fr. Chaumont's father found the strength to leave his bed and was driven to the church to attend Mass and receive Holy Communion. He died a few days later.

Before the priest moved on to other assignments, he was given another responsibility in the parish of Saint Marcel. In 1868 the administration had eliminated the position of resident priest at the hospital of La Salpêtrie: this responsibility was added to the work of the clergy of Saint Marcel.

Beginning as a Spiritual Director

In his biography of Henri Chaumont, Msgr. Laveille provides two examples of the beginning of the young priest's work as a spiritual director at Saint Marcel, taken from his experiences with women from very different backgrounds.

The countess of Tury was a member of high society sent to Fr. Chaumont by Msgr. de Ségur with great confidence. The younger priest advised her to follow a path inspired by the writings of St. Francis de Sales.

He asked her first to read the Gospels and the lives of the saints in order to strengthen her faith and abandon the prejudices that separated true Christian practice from a worldly life. He did not hesitate to speak harshly to her about her way of life.

The people you meet, now and earlier, in your level of society have given you an intellectual pride that men like to display in the name of a liberal mind. Many women cultivate the same mentality, calling it a faith that is moderate and enlightened. In fact, it is nothing more than a dying faith and a warming-over of the intellectual sophistication of the last century.[43]

He heard lukewarm Christians say, self-righteously, that people had abused the sense of devotion, that piety transplanted from the cloister cannot survive the poisonous atmosphere of the real world; that the Gospel, though of course it is true, should be adapted charitably and reasonably to our present difficulties either by tolerance for evil or acceptance of human weakness.

These contemporary Christians, partly out of respect for others' opinions and wanting to avoid conflict, partly through indifference or looking for an easier path in society, began to say the same things, and without realizing it, to think them. This is a sad obstacle to the establishment of true piety in a soul. It does not matter if human wisdom is shocked or worldly Christians are indignant. I will say, and

---

[43]He is reproaching her for accepting the "spirit of the Enlightenment" professing insidiously a certain scorn for religious practice judged by individual reason.

proclaim all my life that such a spirit is not compatible with the practice of the Gospel, even in worldly society. God does not reveal himself to the wise and the cautious, but to the humble and the meek.[44]

Fr. Chaumont was following St. Francis de Sales in denouncing the accepted idea, reinforced by the Enlightenment, that religious devotion belongs only in the cloister: the morality preached in the Gospels is "heroic," not practicable in society. The opposite was a fundamental truth for Henri Chaumont. As a spiritual guide, he proposed this program of readings:

We can begin a serious and useful conversation with the Exercises of Saint Ignatius and the Confessions of Augustine, then come to the Introduction to the Devout Life followed by some beautiful treatises or sermons by Saint Thomas Aquinas, on the subject of holy Charity; then to form the soul for personal devotion, Saint Bernard and Saint Alphonsus Liguori[45] *who*

---

[44] A letter dated August 7, 1869, quoted by Msgr. Laveille. The assertions that Fr. Chaumont denounces are indeed in the spirit of the editors of the *Encyclopaedia,* Diderot and d'Alembert. The morality of the Gospels certainly seems, for most people, impossible to practice. St. Francis de Sales proposes a doctrine completely opposed to this attitude. Devotion and a life following the Gospel are possible for all. That is why the *Introduction to the Devout Life* is among the first readings that Fr. Chaumont suggested in spiritual direction.

[45] The reference is probably to a work by St. Alphonsus Ligouri, *Les Glories de Marie,* which was widely read in the nineteenth century.

speak so beautifully of the Holy Virgin, with Saint Theresa, and Saint Joseph, to follow.[46]

These choices on the part of Fr. Chaumont are significant: The *Exercises* of Ignatius are intended to lead to a "choice," the choice of a new way of life. The *Confessions* show by concrete example that such a conversion is possible; St. Francis de Sales demonstrates that the saintly life is not only meant for heroes, something that St. Augustine's life might suggest, but that it is offered to all of us.

Miss Loiseau was an employee at the post office, who had to care for her invalid father, and lived with an uncle whose thoughts were far from the Church. Beyond her individual case, it is possible to glimpse a "type" of Catholic that was widespread at the time.

She brought to her confessor an honest and delicate soul, capable of higher aspirations, but lacking balance and discipline in her spiritual life.[47] She could be too scrupulous in her examination of conscience and inclined to "philosophize" the questions of doctrine that troubled her. She needed encouragement and guidance, but especially authority. Fr. Chaumont supported her patiently and gently in her struggle, and especially helped her to find the strength she needed to make lasting progress. (Msgr. Laveille)

---

[46] Chaumont, unpublished letter dated August 26, 1869, quoted by Msgr. Laveille.

[47] The choice of words by the monsignor suggests that Miss Loiseau was perhaps uncontrollably emotional in her faith from time to time.

He invited her to find the spirit of Jesus within, that is, to find peace tempered with fervor and inward calm. He defined these qualities this way:

The spirit of Jesus is not the spirit of servile fear that perturbs the heart; it is the spirit of a peaceful love, leading us to observe the law, not through obligation but by choice, finding in it infinite consolation.

Fervor is simply a readiness of spirit and heart to act in God's service. We do not compare the fervent soul to the tortoise but to the eagle who flies rapidly and seeks out the regions of the sky that are closest to the sun. Fervor, once again, is not a feverish spirit. . . . The soul that is nourished by the world and agitation is consumed by a constant fever. But the faithful soul that is nourished by the earthly paradise of Christian virtues flies upward with agility, in spiritual peace.

Meditation? It is the state of the soul that is always self-possessed, giving choices in the exterior world only the minimum of attention. It uses the contemporary world as a vehicle to bring it to God. [48]

Fr. Chaumont seemed more positive with this woman who was so questioning, sometimes tormented by scruples, but who had already begun her spiritual journey, than in his relationship with the Countess de Tury, who was still hesitant to undertake the journey. He wanted to bring her to spiritual peace, but encourage her to make progress in giving herself to

---

[48] Letter dated May 26, 1866, in the volume *Spiritual Letters* of Fr. Chaumont [If this is part of title, make it ital.].

God. In his abundant advice to her, there seem to be hints that he was reading Teresa of Avila.

Fr. Chaumont intended to form the first group of young women, including Miss Loiseau, who would begin the study of Francis de Sales. But, as we will see in Chapter V, he could not follow through with this project. At the same time, suffering from an attack of acute arthritis, he made a vow to make a pilgrimage to Annecy (June 1868), which will be discussed later in this biography. At the end of October, he published the first volume of his *Spiritual Direction Following the Teachings of Saint Francis de Sales.*

Having succeeded brilliantly in his examinations for young priests, Henri Chaumont was sent to a new position as assistant at Sainte Clotilde. (December 1868)

CHAPTER III

ASSISTANT AT SAINTE CLOTILDE IN
TROUBLED TIMES (1868-1874)

The new assignment may have appeared to be a promotion for Henri Chaumont, but he did not see it that way. In his ministry he maintained the same demands on his own person and the same devotion to the flock that was confided to him, no matter how different they were from the parishioners of Saint Marcel. He became better known and the nature of his evangelization more clearly defined.

Sainte Clotilde, The Parish

It is difficult to imagine a greater contrast than that between the parish Fr. Henri Chaumont left behind in 1868 and his new one. Sainte Clotilde is in one of the most aristocratic parts of Paris, on the left bank of the Seine, with large private houses separated from the street by courtyards, with beautiful gardens in the rear.

The parish of 17,000 members was formed by the consolidation in 1856–1857 of two parishes, Sainte Valère and Abbaye au Bois. The new church, finished in 1865, was one of the first in France to be built in the neo-Gothic style, considered at the time to be a mark of prestige.

Fr. Pierre-Ambroise Hamelin (1800–1883), formerly the assistant at the Abbaye au Bois, was named pastor of the consolidated parish. Already quite old, with an austere demeanor, he was nevertheless especially gentle with children. He wanted to continue his work with catechism, visiting the sick, preaching, and hearing confessions. He insisted, with a certain degree of pomp, on beauty and elegance in the Liturgy. At the same time he wanted to found a school for boys and one for girls. He had twelve priests at his service; among them Fr. Chaumont ranked near the bottom, after the two primary assistants, Frs. Léré and Vanhaelst. Within the parish there was a high percentage of practicing Catholics as Fr. Chaumont himself described:

Easter in this parish is especially beautiful. We have been hearing confessions continually for fifteen days, preparing the faithful for their Easter duty. There have been many conversions. I think that twelve thousand of our seventeen thousand parishioners received communion at Easter. You can imagine how happy we were.[49]

At the time, assistants and lesser clergy did not live in the same residence; Fr. Chaumont had to find lodging in the area. He was delighted to live near Msgr. de Ségur, whom he could visit frequently. He immediately accepted the duty to celebrate the 6:00 a.m. daily Mass, where he found himself again with domestics and workers ready to hear the simple words of instruction he was accustomed to delivering at Saint Marcel. In lively catechism classes, he returned to the methods of Saint Sulpice that he had used as a seminarian.

---

[49]Henri Chaumont's letter to a parishioner at Saint-Marcel, April 2, 1869, quoted by Msgr. Laveille.

The instruction was always clear, precise, and well organized. No wandering from the topic, nothing vague. The children understood easily so that they could write clearly about each topic he presented. The comments that Fr. Chaumont wrote on each of the compositions brought joy to the pupils. As he called roll, the priest made subtle, sometimes mischievous reflections on his young charges, but he was always respectful and gentle, so that there were often nearly imperceptible smiles on the faces of the children.[50]

On the other hand, given the intellectual level of these parishioners, he no longer preached from a few simple notes as he had done at Saint Marcel. He wrote out his homilies and collected them in six notebooks containing no less than 161 texts.

In contrast to the clear and simple exhortations directed toward his working class parishioners, the collection has "a series of historic conversations on devotions in Paris to the Holy Virgin," and a very interesting parallel developed in several lessons, on the Gospel of Christ and the gospel of the world. This preamble summarizes the organization of his project: "The present century, so rich in inventions, flatters itself for having found a new gospel. It does not deny that our Christian Gospel has lofty dogmas, an admirable morality; it gives the example of great virtues. But this century judges that such a Gospel is abstract, and does not apply to the contemporary world. Our contemporaries call it the theoretical gospel. For themselves, they have invented the

---

[50]Memories of catechism by Mme Jules Aubert, quoted by Msgr. Laveille.

practical gospel. However, behind this rhetoric there are some important facts. We are in the presence of two gospels, and each one claims to provide answers for personal salvation, the salvation of the family and society. We will compare them, examining their origins and their opposing dogmas. (Msgr. Laveille)

Here then we find the differences between the Gospel morality and that of "living correctly," which they claim should satisfy members of contemporary society.

Those who heard it remember a discourse that immediately captured the attention and awakened the reflection of those who heard it, addressing the mind and the will more than the emotions, intending to convince and persuade rather than to touch the emotions. If the emotions come into play, it is not the desired effect, but a secondary result of the intent to act on the listeners, for fear that words may be powerless and the word of God may fall on a soil that has been badly prepared. (Msgr. Debout)

In his book Msgr. Laveille gave several examples of the untiring devotion of the young Fr. Chaumont: on one occasion he offered to replace one of his fellow priests who had been called to take the last sacraments to a man dying of small pox.[51] He also tells how Fr. Chaumont's expression of faith brought a convinced

---

[51]Black small pox, extremely contagious and mortal, for which a vaccination was perfected by the Englishman Edward Jenner in 1796.

follower of Voltaire back to the Church as he was facing death.

Confessor

As he had done at Saint Marcel, Fr. Chaumont devoted a major part of his time to spiritual guidance. He himself wrote:

Here is how I usually spend my time: Monday, Wednesday and Thursday, I am at the church from 7:00 to 9:00 a.m., from 1:00 to 6:00 in the afternoon, the whole day Saturday, and Sunday between celebrating Masses. Tuesday and Friday are for running errands farther from the parish or for remaining at home.[52]

A woman for whom he was spiritual guide (Miss Toneri) gives a slightly different perspective:

At Sainte Clotilde he always said the 6:00 Mass and before leaving the sacristy he waited for the first stroke of the hour before going to the chapel where he would officiate. During this interval the chapel where he heard confessions began to fill. After the holy office he went directly to the confessional. About 8:00 a.m. his sister Marthe came to bring his breakfast. Our devoted Fr. took five minutes out. He continued hearing confessions till 11:00, and began again at 2:00 p.m. Often at 6:00 p.m. the sacristan was waiting to close the church, keys in hand, until the last person left the

---

[52]An unpublished letter from a parishioner, dated July 17, 1869, quoted by Msgr. Laveille. This would make a total of thirty-two hours of Confessions each week, comparable to the number of hours Fr. Chaumont spent hearing Confessions at Saint Marcel.

confessional. The priest heard the confessions of ladies of society and poor servants; he showed no preference, but if he saw a man waiting for confession, he heard him right away.[53]

He united the Sacrament of Penance with spiritual guidance, no doubt following the ideas of his friend, Fr. Rérérony, who explained the advantages of combining two acts that are by their nature separate.

It seems to me that a confessor who is only a confessor limits himself to examining whether the person who comes to him should receive absolution; he offers an exhortation that more or less corresponds to the actions of the contrite listener, gives him a penance once again more or less adequate to his or her needs, and sends the person back to the same spiritual context as before. The confessor who is also a spiritual director not only hears the sins revealed and judges them. He also tries cautiously to enter the heart of the person who speaks, to understand this life, these habits and penchants, and insofar as he can, understand a whole human being. He tries to find the weakness, the principal lack, and then the virtue toward which the grace of God inclines this soul. In response to these faults and this virtue he provides counsel that is personal and practical; he organizes the combat, suggests measures to be taken, strengthened by some

---

[53]*Summarium*. This remark concerning men leads us to think that there were many fewer men confessing and that Fr. Chaumont did not want to keep them waiting, perhaps because he considered that they had taken time away from their work, or perhaps because he did not want to see men and women mingled in the line.

little sacrifices, that challenge and nourish the generosity that waits there, rather than exhausting it or discouraging it. He will see the weakness of the will. But this director prefers and soon uses only penances that are medicinal. [54]

The spiritual director has a plan of action that he tries to put in place for each soul that he has in his care. Each confession is a step toward this goal, an effort in this direction. The advice or the penances that he gives or practices that he suggests, Communions that he permits, all the relationships that he has with this soul are coherent, one leading to the next. For the confessor who is only a confessor the confessions are each an independent act. Confession, if it is only that, is a medicine applied and if necessary, reapplied in the same way. Spiritual direction is a sustaining regimen. [55]

It is clear that Révérony, Chaumont, and other like-minded priests called "Liguorian," preferred to combine spiritual direction with confession, so that they accompanied each soul beyond the pardon of sins and encouraged the spiritual progress of the faithful.

As a result of the misadventure at Saint Marcel, Fr. Chaumont took every precaution when hearing the

---

[54]It was customary at that time to distinguish between "punitive" and "medicinal" penances. The former seem like a fine paid for a wrong action; the latter like remedies intended to heal a penchant for sin.

[55]Letter from Fr. Révérony to Fr. Chaumont, January 10, 1868, quoted by Msgr. Laveille.

confessions of women.[56] Entering his confessional in the chapel of Sainte Valère, he maintained an austere demeanor, indicating not only his respect for the Sacrament of Reconciliation, but also the respect he wanted to inspire for the priesthood. He refused to shake hands with women and asked them to keep a certain distance from him. Msgr. Debout described him in this way:

His reserve was absolute. He feared all familiarity; that may be why even within his family he did not seem to seek out the company of little children. In his relationships with women he never wanted to take their hand, even if they were older and well known for their piety. To avoid having to accept a hand that was offered, he occupied his own hand with his breviary or his hat, which sometimes caused embarrassment or humiliation but Fr. Chaumont was faithful to this perfect prudence to the end. (Msgr. Debout)[57]

In his spiritual direction he combined rigorous method and gentleness in the procedure he recommended.

It seems that rigor would also be the guiding spirit of his work as confessor, even to excess. It was known

---

[56]Nevertheless, a woman whose spiritual director was Fr. Chaumont told a story of a male relative of another woman, whose confessor was also Fr. Chaumont. The point of the story was to imply that the woman stayed too long in the confessional. Although the man tried to surprise the priest in wrongdoing, his plot failed. The priest was ultimately able to reconcile the relative with the faith, visiting him during a serious illness.

[57]It was noticed that in these matters Fr. Chaumont was more prudent than the norm for clergy at the time.

that he first required a general confession[58] from each person who sought progress in spiritual life and renunciation of a number of tendencies whose dangers the person had previously not seen. After some time, the person would understand the purpose of Fr. Chaumont's exhortations: to free the soul from itself and to direct it lovingly toward Jesus. He did not try simply to empty the heart that turned to him for counsel; he invited it to reject false and disappointing idols and put in their place the divine Guest, the infallible principle of spiritual happiness.

Moreover, in order to encourage those in his spiritual care to make sacrifices, he knew how to speak with gentleness that touched the heart; he was compassionate in the face of any distress. These souls received the joy of being rapidly and completely understood. This was due to the priest's extraordinary gift of observation, which continued to develop with every passing day. (Msgr. Laveille) [59]

In this description by one of the priest's protégées, Marie-Agnes Tessier, the words *patience, gentleness,* and *encouragement* are a strong indication of the Salesian thread in his thought:

Fr. Chaumont was always perfectly punctual at his confessional; he was careful to treat all who came to

---

[58]The confession should take into consideration as much of one's past life as it is possible to recall.

[59]When Fr. Chaumont first began direction with a soul truly committed to advancing in the spiritual life, he was rigorous, even severe, trying to bring about serious change. He adapted his guidance to correspond to the needs of this soul, but always with the goal of bringing about a deep attachment to Christ.

him with untiring patience and gentleness. He tried with gradual and gentle measures to awaken in his parishioners a serious and constant quest for holiness. . . . Seeing only the interest of those souls entrusted to him, he made no distinction between a duchess and her servants, and maintained his freedom as an apostle to recall everyone to their duties as Christians.

He was always encouraging and paternal in the Sacrament of Reconciliation, opening souls to receive healing for their hidden suffering. Anyone whose spiritual guidance he accepted was in his eyes predestined for holiness, a person whose supernatural future was in his hands and whose progress he was bound to encourage. (Summarium)

Bishop Debout outlined the major aspects of his spiritual direction this way:

Following the method of St. Francis de Sales, he asked of all who came to him a special effort to arrive at a perfectly pure conscience. He worked to break down pride, to keep thought turned toward God through appropriate reading and the love of mortification through the contemplation of the crucified Christ. Often he even suggested the prudent use of penitential instruments.

He devoted himself fully to each soul that God sent to him, interested in all the details of their spiritual life without ever descending to minutia or puerility.

He had insights and discernment that allowed him to penetrate rapidly to people's inner paths; he revealed people to themselves. He could show them God's purposes for their lives and find the ways that grace could touch them, using their very own qualities as a lever to raise them toward God's love.[60]

If he found greater consolation working with generous souls and asked much of them, he offered the same goodness to weak ones, to those who are painful for a confessor. He had as well a special gift of working with the over-scrupulous. He did not discourage them; he showed them tireless patience and understanding, consoled them, and reassured them with as much gentleness as authority.[61]

On several occasions Fr. Chaumont explained what he himself meant by "spiritual direction." In the following text, clearly from a later period in his life, he delineates how best to deal with the different types of spiritual needs he encountered so that he could provide each soul with goals that could be met:

To guide a soul, that is to meet it where it is in its spiritual journey, with its imperfections, even its sins, to lead it where you as confessor want it to be, that is, grounded in the love of God, progressing not in a single bound but by degrees: first the stage of

---

[60]Fr. Chaumont did not try to shape a soul against its nature or shock it. His goal was to build on the inner attraction toward God that he found already present in a soul who came to him.

[61]The expression "weak souls" probably referred to those who fell frequently into the same errors, apparently making no progress. The scrupulous, on the other hand, have a tendency to feel guilty about everything. Their need is to be reassured so that they do not give in to despair but also to discern what in their conduct might actually lead them in to sin.

compunction,[62] *then shame for the sins committed, further, to the desire to be converted, then to observation of Christ's precepts, and finally to piety, using all the discretion that the Gospel provides.*

The first measure, and the easiest, is simply to apply the rules of moral theology: assume the authority that helps to guide a soul to live a Christian life. This guidance can be given even to those who receive the sacraments once a year, at Easter. From such Catholics the spiritual director must ask for a promise to be faithful in prayer or require some specific practice of piety. From those who receive Communion three or four times a year, the spiritual director can ask for more; he must ask them to sanctify the duties and the pains of daily life. True spiritual direction can begin when the priest has found the dominant weakness in this soul, because it is useless to build until one is certain of what has first to be torn down.

After a time, the priest can impose, with great discretion, a regimen composed of only one or two elements, but that can be increased little by little. This is the best way to guarantee perseverance and lay the foundation of the search for perfection.

True spiritual direction lies in the application of the rules of mystical theology: this is continuous and structured action toward the goal of Christian perfection. To undertake this, the priest needs more developed knowledge, familiarity with different

---

[62]This word for Henri Chaumont and his time evoked a certain sadness caused by the realization that one has "missed the mark" that God wants for us.

methods of prayer, such as meditative, discursive, conversational. It requires affection, union, contemplation.[63]

The priest can simply require those who commune once a year a faithfulness to Christian moral precepts and regular prayer, which helps to sustain fidelity. To souls whose spiritual life is already stronger, the director proposes a daily "re-reading" of their life through examination of conscience, which shows them the path of progress. Fr. Chaumont emphasizes the importance of providing spiritual direction to children:

It is easy to correct the young, to form their natures, and if, in these young souls there is, thank God, nothing that would require making a confession, there are qualities that can be guided. Even a mother who accepts her duty as a Christian to shape her child's moral sense is generally grateful for the additional guidance of a priest. Such direction is easy because a child is not defiant, is forthright, and loves God by his or her very nature. One should not deform their spirit, rather questioning them clearly without letting them get confused in their explanations. One should never be severe, because if a child's first confession inspires fear, that feeling will persist and close that heart forever.

A boy of eight or ten is sufficiently mature to hear practical direction concerning his weakness and his most important good qualities. The priest can direct him by God's love if the child is generous and

---

[63]Spoken at the retreat of Athis, taken from the report quoted by Msgr. Debout.

courageous; if he has a more reflective and reasoning character, he can be shown what things are evil. It is more difficult to deal with young girls because they are timid and it is more difficult to question them. We must touch their hearts through God's love, and avoid exaggerated emotionality. In sum, as Msgr. de Ségur advises, reveal more of Jesus to children, more than is regularly done in catechism classes.[64]

In this advice, which indicates the priest's experience of several years, the last sentence indicates that he was dissatisfied with the catechism teaching methods of his time, in the form of question-and-response, which he believed to be too conceptual to bring the child into contact with the person of Jesus.

The Siege of Paris and the Commune

The Franco-Prussian War marked the brutal end of the Second Empire, which was apparently considered so brilliant an age. It was begun by the blunders of the French government, on August 2, 1870. It was, in fact, a series of defeats for France leading to the fall of the Empire and, on September 4, the proclamation of the Third Republic. At Sainte Clotilde, Fr. Chaumont was witness to the different phases of the war. At first he saw officers and soldiers rushing *en masse* to receive the sacraments. As the defeats began, he had to console his parishioners who had lost loved ones:

There is so much to do here, encouraging so many spouses and mothers, grieving the loss of what was

---

[64]Notes taken at the meetings that took place May 27 and June 30, 1881, quoted by Msgr. Debout.

dearest to them, the men who were immolated near Wissembourg.[65] *Days go by and we can do nothing else. In general, here in Paris we are in a state of panic, exposed on all sides: we fear that we will have a civil war along with the foreign war. May God protect France!*[66]

On September 4 the Empire was overthrown and the Republic proclaimed. The Prussian siege of Paris began on September 19. Fr. Chaumont added a new responsibility to his usual duties:

[He] was accepted to serve as a priest with the mobile hospitals,[67] *organized on rue Saint Dominique, under*

---

[65]On August 4, 1870, the brigade of Abel Douay was surprised by the Bavarian and Prussian vanguards at the frontier city of Wissembourg. The French were defeated, outnumbered one to four against the enemy.

[66]Letter of Fr. Chaumont dated August 11, 1870, in *Spiritual Letters*. While many Parisians nursed the illusion of a quick victory, Fr. Chaumont, closer to the personal anguish caused by the conflict, was a better judge of the calamity and the fragility of the political regime. As a resident of a middle-class area of the city, he certainly heard the rumors spread about the working classes in Belleville, Ménilmontant, Montmartre, and Clignancourt, who were quick to rise in discontent. Beginning in the autumn, the partisans of Blanqui, the socialist revolutionary from Belleville, declared their intention to take over in Paris with the name of "the Commune." On October 31, the rebels were nearly ready to take power at (city hall) the seat of Paris government, Hôtel de Ville.

[67]These were in fact improvised hospitals for wounded soldiers. Authors writing at that time described their lack of organization but also commented on the charity poured out for them. The Christian Brothers often served as stretcher carriers on the combat fronts.

the Ministry of War. Soon he could be seen wearing the armband of the Geneva Convention[68] and the black beard, which indicated to the soldiers that he was one of them, crisscrossing the rooms where men injured by gunshot wounds lay side by side with those consumed by fever or tuberculosis.

Serving as a priest in a military hospital presented some very particular difficulties. These same men who, under fire and facing death, asked for absolution, perhaps crying from their very heart, once they were crowded together away from the front, surrounded by silent, expressionless comrades, no longer dared to give a sign of their faith. If the priest wanted to speak with them of God, he had to lower his voice, and it was almost impossible to hear a confession in secret; with beds so close together, no intimacy was possible.

First he had to get to know these men from such different backgrounds; some wanted to see nothing more in the priest than a likable comrade, well-educated and kind. To move beyond this acceptance to be recognized as a priest, he had to be lovable as a man.

The austere appearance that Fr. Henri Chaumont showed in his relationships with women would have worked against him if he had not known how to soften it from time to time. But from his first days in the hospital he found the appropriate approach: his manner was more relaxed, his expression alert, his voice gentle and nuanced, with a ready smile, even a hint of irony; his conversation was witty and engaging.

---

[68]That is, the Red Cross.

Everything in his demeanor suggested a Parisian of good family, who effortlessly became the understanding friend of the wounded trooper. Thus when he appeared in the wards, there was an outpouring of good humor. Nearly always his hand, extended in friendship, became the hand granting absolution. (Msgr. Laveille)

On January 28, after 135 days of siege, the city fell. But another danger was waiting: civil war. A National Assembly was elected on February 8, 1871, and a preliminary peace treaty signed at Versailles. On February 26, 1871, a movement rose against the peace initiatives: it was the Commune of Paris, which the government of Adolphe Thiers struggled against.[69] On April 5, 1871, the Communards published their decree, announcing hostages taken: Archbishop Darboy and a vicar general, Fr. Lagarde, as well as Fr. Deguerry, pastor of the church of the Madeleine and other priests and religious. Fr. Lagarde was able to escape, but Msgr. Darboy and Fr. Deguerry were shot

---

[69]Whereas the Republicans were more numerous in Paris, the Assembly was mostly conservative (400 monarchists of the 675 members). Fearing the popular uprising in Paris, the Assembly decided to move its seat to Versailles, which evoked an unfortunate symbol. One of its first measures was to end the salaries paid to the national guard, a salary that provided a minimum of income for unemployed workers. However, the national guard had kept its arms (300,000 rifles and 227 cannons). The attempt to recover these cannons from Belleville and Montmartre marked the beginning of the Commune. Thiers's government left Paris for Versailles while the insurgents formed a Central Committee on March 6 and adopted a program of action, (red flag, separation of Church and state). The "Communards " numbered about 30,000.

in the prison of La Roquette. On May 26, forty-nine people, including thirty-three Republican Guards, two policemen and nine priests were shot on rue Haxo, at the top of rue Ménilmontant, one of the last strongholds of the Communards, cornered by the "Army of Versailles." The Commune decided that every Frenchman less than forty years old remaining in Paris should be enlisted in the "Army of the Confederated." At Sainte Clotilde only three priests remained, the two oldest and one Belgian. The pastor and the others had left the church in disguise. Fr. Chaumont was faced with the alternative of following their example or being forced to take up arms against his fellow countrymen. After some hesitation, he decided to leave the capital. He wrote:

It is an honor to be imprisoned because you are a priest; to be shot for the same reason would be glorious, but to carry a rifle to support the Commune against legitimate order, that is to side with the Devil against God; that would be a crime. And as the Devil knows very well, this is the kind of war carried out against the clergy in order to get rid of us. Not having the happiness to be imprisoned or shot, I have gone away for a few days. I am near Orléans along the train route waiting for the moment when the Communards can no longer apply their infamous law and I can return to Paris, even if I have to face the other consequences. Pray with me that this exile ends quickly.[70]

---

[70]Letter to Mme Carré de Malberg, April 12, 1871, quoted by Msgr. Laveille.

He found refuge at La Chapelle Saint Meslin, with the uncle of Miss Loiseau, who had found work with the local post office. The minor seminary of Orléans is also located in this village. But Fr. Chaumont wanted to be closer to where he could be useful; he left for Versailles hoping to return to Paris with the army. Since the city was overwhelmed with refugees, he had to leave for the country house of its priest, Fr. Hamelin. He was welcomed cordially for a month-long stay. Meanwhile, his mother and sisters had been able to leave Paris and find refuge with a friend of the family in the region of Sarthe, near the Loire River. From there they were able to maintain regular correspondence with Henri.

But the priest was uneasy staying so far from the parish he had been forced to leave, so he decided to return to Paris *incognito.* He went first to Saint Denis but the situation became worse: it was the third week of May 1871. On May 24, the first troops of the Army of Versailles entered the city provoking the massacre of the hostages and the burning of the principal monuments of Paris, the Tuileries, the Palais Royal, and the Hôtel de Ville. Fr. Chaumont, disguised as a coal vender, found a man who agreed to take him back to Paris for an exorbitant sum. After a trip lasting twenty-six hours, he was back in his parish. (Note: Today this is a distance covered in forty-five minutes by Metro.) His nephew said that in order to insure his disguise, the priest even carried a sack of coal.

If the material destruction was in fact less than the newspapers first announced, the moral damage was much more serious. The Commune was a true civil war; the wounds were very slow to heal: on one side, killing the hostages; on the other, shooting the insurgents, the "Fédérés," against the wall of the Père Lachaise Cemetery. Fr. Chaumont was an eyewitness:

One morning a group came in haste to call the priests from Sainte Clotilde to perform the last rites for Msgr. Darboy; his body, bloody and unrecognizable, had been brought to the residence of the Archbishop. Fr. Chaumont was shaken by this frightening spectacle. The doctor who examined the wounds declared without hesitation that the prelate had been thrown into the common grave while he was still breathing. The index finger of his right hand, broken by a bullet, indicated that he had fallen while blessing his executioners. Fr. Chaumont had always spoken of his great respect for Msgr. Darboy but regretted his "liberal illusions."[71] Faced with this cadaver mutilated by an enraged crowd, he recalled the gentle observation pronounced by the archbishop as the insurgents led him away: "I have always loved liberty." But the response of these savages was "Your liberty is not the same as ours." (Msgr. Laveille)

This spectacle, nevertheless, did not move Fr. Chaumont to change his unfavorable opinion of liberalism and Gallicanism[72] in the Church, which the Archbishop had professed.

---

[71]On this point he shares the views of Msgr. de Ségur. (See the following chapter.)

[72]Catholic liberalism in the mid-nineteenth century is better described as a current of ideas rather than a doctrine. It encouraged Catholics to see the parliamentary regime in a

Asked what he hoped for in the successor to Archbishop Darboy, the vicar of Sainte Clotilde replied, "We pray God will give us an archbishop who is fully Roman and filled with the spirit of Our Lord." At other times he encouraged his priests to combat the spirit of revolution, which surfaced nearly everywhere, and he noted with satisfaction that the Society of Priests of St. Francis de Sales helped its members react against this spirit.[73]

These ideas did not diminish the priest's compassion toward one of the insurgents of the Commune. This episode shows clearly the tension that weighed on Paris in the wake of the civil war.

On one occasion, during his service at Saint Marcel, Fr. Chaumont climbed several flights of stairs to visit a family faced with many domestic problems. The husband greeted him with this tirade: "Father, I know that you have helped my wife and my children, that you are a good man, so I welcome you to my home in spite of the habit you are wearing. But if you were only a priest, all the hatred I feel for your Church would fall on you and I wouldn't be satisfied until I had pushed you down the stairs." The priest was faced with a worker who was intelligent, who had even studied, but his attitude was misdirected. His ideology was fundamentally honest, but he had heard and believed

---

positive light and to encourage the Church to position itself in this political framework. "Néo-gallicanisme" in the nineteenth century resisted the movement, calling on the French Church to adopt "Italian" piety and to give a greater role to the magisterium, a movement known as "ultramontanism,"
[73]Texts quoted by Msgr. Debout.

the lies of socialists, who although they were in good faith, saw the Church as their worst enemy.[74]

Some weeks later the insurrection broke out. In spite of his wife's tears, the unfortunate man became an officer in the insurgent army. He was captured and, together with his band of insurgents, imprisoned at Satory, where he had to wait with a mixture of anger and bitterness until military justice had the time to hear his case.

How to shorten this unbearable wait? His wife, knowing the generosity of Fr. Chaumont, pleaded with him to try to hasten the trial date. The commission for classification of hearings at the Minister of War was Lieutenant Colonel Carré, who had acquired a true respect for his wife's spiritual director. Through him, Fr. Chaumont was able to advance the examination of the case.

The priest's goodness touched the Communard deeply. He had been taken advantage of in the formation of his ideas; he was not perverse. Moreover, he had changed his opinion of the Fédérés, when he saw how basely they had behaved in the course of events. He said as much to Fr. Chaumont as he thanked him for lessening the anxiety of his wife and children.

Soon the former insurgent was called before the tribunal, scheduled for October 11, in the new factory at Sèvres. His case was serious: it was widely known what the sentence was for officers of the Fédérés taken

---

[74]This hatred of the clergy was widespread among revolutionary socialists at the time.

with their arms in hand. The accused, little by little finding his former convictions weakened by all of the evidence of Fr. Chaumont's generosity, begged him to help him at the hearing. He reminded the priest that there was more than one life hanging in the balance; Fr. Chaumont had the presentiment that an eternal soul depended on his resolution. He accepted.

The day arrived. The Parisian priest, unknown in Sèvres, took his seat on the bench of the defense with the obvious intention to save one of the leaders of the insurgency from the death penalty that had up until then been summarily handed down by the military commission.

First, he cleverly presented the circumstances that had influenced his client, his training, an indoctrination that he was not equipped to counter. He described his irreproachable past life, his refusal to participate in the worst orgies of violence committed by the rebels, his loyal service as a worker, all of this without trying to suggest that this client was not guilty of participation in the Commune. Such was the story of the legions of accused whom the commission had heard.

The judges received this ingenious defense coldly, too much like so many others they had heard. The priest foresaw the terrible sentence that in spite of everything would close the debate. In a supreme attempt to change the course of the trial, he recalled that these officers had dear ones in their own homes; he implored their pity if not for the man himself who was misguided but guilty, then for his unfortunate wife and children. He conjured up with tears in his voice this family that had been so honorable, whose happiness would sink into shame and terror; this widow and these orphans with no support, condemned to misery, dishonor, and grief without consolation.

As he talked, the faces of the judges softened; a sympathetic attention brightened their expressions; they were moved. The defense could feel that the cause was won. In fact, a few minutes later the commission delivered its verdict of acquittal.

During the hearing, the wife of the accused man was waiting in an adjoining room, extremely anxious. She guessed, seeing the joy on the priest's face, that her husband had been saved. She burst into tears of gratitude. As for the chief of the insurgents who had been saved from death by one of those whom he would gladly have killed some months earlier, he confessed to Fr. Chaumont the details of his errors. He felt a debt, through the priest, to the indulgence of men; from the minister of God he received God's pardon. (Msgr. Laveille)

Fr. Chaumont's ministry continued at Sainte Clotilde. Joining with other militant Catholics of the time, he asked France to repent of her past errors. This was when the decision was made to construct the Basilica of Sacré Coeur (Sacred Heart) in Montmartre. Under the influence of the Comité du Voeux National, and that of the Committee of Moral Order, sessions of the Chamber of Deputies were opened by public prayer, and on June 29, 1873, about fifty Catholic representatives went on a pilgrimage to Paray-le-

Monial[75] with the intention of consecrating France to the Sacred Heart. During the troubles of the Commune, Fr. Chaumont recommended reciting this prayer:

Oh, Mary, conceived without sin, behold France; pray for France, save France. The guiltier she is, the more she needs your intercession. One word from you to Jesus, resting in your arms, and France will be saved. Oh, Jesus, who is obedient to Mary, save our France.

A little later he wrote, *"Who knows what will happen if we do not right the wrong we have done and fail to become a source of edification for the many countries that we have scandalized."*

During the period following the Commune, the Society of Daughters of St. Francis de Sales truly came to be. (See Chapters V and VI.) The founder, conscious of what was at stake, refused the parish proposed to him, as second assistant at Ménilmontant, a densely populated working-class parish in the north of Paris. He considered in effect that his work as spiritual director would be compromised by such a change because the women, whose spiritual journey he had been guiding, could not follow him there.[76] He thought, probably rightly, that he could not undertake

---

[75]The site of a Romanesque basilica in the region of Burgundy (where the Sacred Heart appeared to St. Margaret Mary).

[76]It was not only a question of distance but of the great gap in social position. It is clear that in the context just described, women of high society would not go to meet their spiritual director in one of the largest working-class areas of Paris. Fr. Chaumont chose, then, to refuse a promotion within the clergy in order to continue the project he had undertaken.

again the task of evangelizing among the poor as he had done at Saint Marcel, given the size and socio-economic makeup of Ménilmontant. He asked for another assignment with the excuse that his health was not strong enough for the large parish at Ménilmontant. In the interim he remained at Sainte Clotilde.

Fr. d'Hulst, a fellow student at seminary, who had begun to work with the diocesan administration in March 1872, was also a spiritual son of Msgr. de Ségur. When Fr. Chaumont spoke in confidence to him about his work in spiritual direction, his old friend found a solution that offered a more prestigious position than assistant in a parish but not too onerous: it was that of resident priest at the mother-house of the Christian Brothers on the rue Oudinot. He began work there on October 15, 1874, at the age of thirty-six. In spite of his responsibilities toward the brothers, the priest was able to arrange enough independence to allow him to continue his project in spiritual direction at the Benedictine chapel on rue M. le Prince and at the Abaye au Bois, rue de Sèvres. (These are areas of Paris geographically, socially and economically closer to Sainte Clotilde, on the Left Bank.)

CHAPTER IV

MSGR. DE SÉGUR AND HIS INFLUENCE

Having followed the life of Henri Chaumont up to the year 1874, it will be useful now to depart from this chronology and present in detail the lives of two people who played a major role in forming the principal orientations of his life, Msgr. de Ségur and Mme Carré de Malberg. We will look as well at the principal organizations founded by Fr. Chaumont during these years, the Daughters of St. Francis de Sales and the Priests of St. Francis de Sales.

Beginning with his first meeting with Msgr. de Ségur on the evening of his first Communion, Fr. Chaumont felt himself to be a spiritual son of this priest. He sought out his advice and wrote a book commemorating his life.[77] But most of all, the prelate's methods of spiritual direction were a model for Fr. Chaumont.

Monseigneur de Ségur, Student of Francis de Sales

Gaston de Ségur was born April 15, 1820, in Paris, eldest son of Eugène de Ségur and Sophie Rostropchine.[78] According to Gaston de Ségur

---

[77]*Monseigneur de Ségur, Director of Souls,* 1884.

[78]Eugène de Ségur began a military career under the First Empire and continued it during the Restoration. In 1818 he was a lieutenant in the cavalry. The Countess Catherine Rostropchine, wife of a former governor of Moscow and convert to Catholicism, was looking for a husband for her daughter, Sophie, among the Catholic elite at the time. M de Ségur's name was proposed. Mme Swetchine, whose salon was a place for

himself, his conversion took place during the year he passed his baccalaureate exam. Until then, without having lived a dissolute life, he had nevertheless neglected religious practice, except for Easter Communion.

In September 1838, he met two people who would change him: his cousin Augustine Galitzine, a member of the conference of St. Vincent de Paul, whose piety and devotion to the poor touched him deeply, and his maternal grandmother, who did not hesitate to affirm her faith in spite of the opposing currents of the day. The grandmother and her grandson held long conversations about literature that quickly evolved into discussions of religion. Catherine Rostropchine gave Gaston a copy of the *Introduction to the Devout Life*. The young man decided to convert following the model that St. Francis proposes to Philothée. He set the date, September 8, and prepared himself with a retreat nourished by meditations prepared by the bishop of Annecy with the intention of purifying his soul and leading to a "choice," the choice between the life of devotion and a life patterned on worldly values. At the end of the retreat, he made a general confession and received Communion. Following the precepts of St. Francis, he began to commune frequently, at first weekly and then daily.

He began a career as attaché to the embassy in Rome guided by Fr. de Villefort, a Jesuit, and then in the fall of 1843, he entered the seminary at Saint Sulpice. His spiritual director, Msgr. Mollevaut, tempered his

---

meetings and formation for upper-class Catholics of the period, suggested his name to the Countess.

lessons of renunciation and mortification, drawn from the French school of Jean-Jacques Olier and Vincent de Paul, with Salesian gentleness.

We must be careful, he repeated, not to aim so high that the perspective of the road ahead frightens us. Let us go step-by-step, preferring small virtues, following the example of St. Francis de Sales, beginning by accepting ourselves.

Only such Salesian gentleness, in his opinion, could win hearts to the faith. "You will begin to be a spiritual director, he said to his students at La Solitude,[79] when people say of you, 'This is a good man.'" (Marthe de Hédouville)

In his book, Henri Chaumont gathered together the steps for prayer that de Ségur had composed during Henri's last year at seminary. His model is always Jesus Christ, comparing his own miserable condition to the perfection of the Lord.[80] Examining himself in depth, he tried to recognize his own dominant inner tendency, in order to combat it, first of all. After mature reflection, he found that his tendency was vanity, a desire for glory.

---

[79] "La Solitude" is a building belonging to the seminary of Saint Sulpice at Issy-les-Moulineaux, but it refers also to a period in the formation of priests who intended to enter the Company of Saint Sulpice as ministers of spiritual direction.
[80] This spirituality is not far from "néantisation" (seeing yourself as nothing), typical of the French school: become aware of one's own powerlessness and sinfulness in order to better appreciate divine grace.

Having precisely located the old man, he mustered all the efforts of his spiritual life in the struggle against him: prayer, communion, private examination of conscience, penitence, carefully rejecting the impulses and the involuntary imaginings rising in his heart. He then made positive acts of virtue against them, even without any possible pleasure, recalling that he should expect only grace as a recompense. This work of destruction is carried out with a single purpose: to make room for Christ alone. (M de Hédouville)

Fr. de Ségur was ordained a priest December 18, 1847, and then turned his attention to the young people and children of the poor. They included the beggars in the area around Saint Sulpice, idle youths in the Luxembourg Gardens, and the apprentices near Montparnasse. In May 1852 he was called to take the post of auditor at the tribunal of the Rota in Rome. But fate decided otherwise. In 1854 he went blind, probably the result of paralysis of the optic nerve. He had to leave Rome in January 1856. He took an apartment with five rooms at 39 rue du Bac; one room became his chapel. The "blind prelate" devoted himself henceforth to a ministry of confession and spiritual guidance, gaining an extraordinary following for his work. While still in the seminary, Henri Chaumont consulted him about what direction to give his spiritual life. Msgr. de Ségur suggested St. Francis de Sales as his first model:

What caught the attention of the spontaneous nature of the son of the Countess de Ségur was the human quality of Salesian spirituality. No stoicism in the view of St. Francis de Sales, but a tenderness that understood others' pain and deeply felt his own suffering. "He was very emotional," others said of him as they did of Gaston de Ségur. But the emotion of neither man, transformed as it was by saintliness, could be mistaken for sentimentality. Their gentleness and patience was not a sign of weakness, but rather mastery over natures too spontaneous, that harboured anger in Francis de Sales and mockery in Monseigneur de Ségur. (M de Hédouville)

Following the example of St. Francis de Sales, Fr. de Ségur assigned primary importance to the ministry of spiritual direction; "the art of arts," as St. Gregory the Great called it. The director is a guide and a counselor, not a master; those in his spiritual care conserve full freedom of conscience.

Returning time and again to this subject, he cautions priests and the faithful against authoritarianism in spiritual direction. . . . The priest, he said, must not impose his personality. He is not "free in this matter; the Church sets rules . . . that he cannot violate without grave departure from his duty." His role is to discern the truth from illusion, keeping in mind God's actions in each soul. He acts not by giving orders but by advice, even suggestions, that he should be able to present so that the person desires and embraces them. The director never imposes himself; he must know when to withdraw when his role is no longer meaningful. (M de Hédouville)

Fr. de Ségur left an abundant body of work.[81] He wanted his little spiritual treatises to be accessible not only to practicing Christians but also to business people, young people, soldiers, and workers. Here again his vision is aligned with St. Francis de Sales: he intended to "give Jesus to all souls." He was not seeking erudition; he wanted every believer to have an experience of God as love, to taste the goodness of the Lord, to go beyond the moral teachings that were often all that the clergy of his time offered to their flock. Thus, in order to encourage the practice of meditation, he gave his works the general title of *Piety and the Interior Life.* He made a distinction between piety and religion, a distinction common at that time, the former evoking God as a loving father, the latter, God as creator whom we adore from a distance. In order for this piety to bring gentleness, joy, and an open heart, it must be "an ordered, cordial, and affectionate practice," as advocated by the saintly bishop of Geneva.

At the same time, along with Msgr. Olier, Msgr. de Ségur saw renunciation as the Christian's struggle against the "former self," still residing in us and as the action of the soul emptying itself to become pure receptivity, until it is ready to follow in the footsteps of Christ. The Salesian spirit colors this effort with the "human character of saintliness," and softens the severity of "becoming nothing." "Only our sinful *old self* is sacrificed; to lose oneself in God is as sweet as for an infant to abandon itself to the arms of its

---

[81]This nineteenth-century religious author's works reached the widest public.

mother.[82] Henri Chaumont sees the difference between Olier and Francis de Sales in the importance that the latter gives to love of neighbor:

Another characteristic of St. Francis de Sales is love of our fellow human beings. In this he is completely different from Msgr. Olier, who feared the weakness of human nature and, for this reason, sought the emptying out of the heart. He sought to love one's neighbors only in God, through charity and without finding joy in our affection for them. This was not the way of St. Francis. He found pleasure in human friendships, without scruples, but with supernatural love. The richness of his beautiful nature but especially his ardent love for God, the simplicity and purity of his heart, brought him to understand completely how Jesus loved.[83]

Msgr. de Ségur did not hesitate to encourage those he counseled to express the love in their hearts.

How foolish to stifle the expressions of love springing from our hearts, warning that they are dangerous. Where are there not dangers, great God! The heart, good and tender devotion, true love, these are life, and joy, fruitfulness, and happiness. Without this, the priest, whether he is in the confessional, preaching or on his knees before the good Lord, is nothing but an electric light, sterile and cold. We cannot love too much; we never love enough. Who will ever love as

---

[82] Monseigneur de Ségur, *Renunciation*. He is quoting from the *Treatise on the Love of God*, IX, 13.

[83] Talk given by Henri Chaumont at the meeting held November 22, 1880, quoted by Msgr. Debout

much as Jesus loved? Jesus is in us, to transfigure us, to make us like him, to make our hearts his own heart, loving adorably. But we must love as he loves, with him, never without him. To love without him is to love against him, in fact, to lose true love.[84]

St. Francis de Sales was the source for the images that Msgr. de Ségur used to express Christ's presence in the soul:

His personal experience is witness to the infinite sweetness we can feel as the divine presence enters us, leading us to want to be like Jesus; "we cannot help imitating what we love." He has a beautiful way of speaking of Christ's welcoming love, leading the soul to a filial abandonment, but not passivity; it encourages us to seek knowledge of God with the help of our natural reason.

"[God has] planted a good tree in us . . . and its fruits will be good."

We will perform acts of the will to keep ourselves attentive to our inner Guest, to master our natural impressions, to be patient with others and ourselves. (M de Hédouville)

Fr. de Ségur puts the person of Jesus at the center; Christ is present in every Christian.

He encouraged frequent Communion, countering the influence of Jansenism.[85] For those who came to him

---

[84] Msgr. de Ségur, letter written December 3, 1868.

[85] His work titled "Most Holy Communion" (1860) was a great success; 180,000 copies were sold in six years, and the 77th

for spiritual direction, he encouraged the habit of mental prayer (a half-hour at the beginning of the day). In this way, following the teachings of Francis de Sales, it is possible to maintain a peaceful heart, the peace that comes from giving oneself over to the will of God.

Monseigneur de Ségur and Father Chaumont

The two men met when the young priest was living in the community on rue Cassette. The young boy, Henri, made his first Communion June 21, 1850, at the church of Saint Sulpice. They found a real affinity for each other, especially at the time that the child was experiencing his spiritual crisis. Msgr. Debout told of a lighter moment between the two: Fr. de Ségur was Henri's spiritual director. The boy accused himself of some mischief, while he was still in the grip of scrupulosity. Fr. de Ségur responded, "Lies like that, I'll allow you eleven a day, but not one more, understand?"

A little later Fr. de Ségur was able to take advantage of his friendship with Msgr. Pie, bishop of Poitiers, to have Henri accepted at the minor seminary in Montmorillon, assuring him of an excellent education.

---

edition was published in 1891. Nevertheless, the book provoked controversy and some priests went so far as to denounce it from the pulpit. The spirituality of Msgr. de Ségur was at odds with the pastoral rigor derived from the Jansenism current in France during the eighteenth and the beginning of the nineteenth centuries. In the spirit of Jansenism, Communion was a reward for a Christian who had overcome sin. For Msgr. de Ségur, "we commune not because we are good, but in order to become better."

It also allowed the young man to take advantage of the retreats preached by the "blind prelate." Msgr. de Ségur invited the young man to give his whole heart to Jesus. Henri Chaumont responded to him in this way:

The day of my first Communion, I received two remarkable graces from God: he gave me his only begotten Son and introduced me to one of his great servants. These two graces probably cannot be compared, if we look at the splendor of Jesus and the nothingness of his priest.

Msgr. de Ségur, then Fr. de Ségur, immediately and better than anyone else revealed to my soul the Jesus that I understood so little. I have had the consolation of knowing many saintly priests. I am grateful to them for their devotion and their excellent advice. But when I wanted to understand Jesus, at the age of twelve, of fifteen, or twenty, find in Christian teaching the spirit of Jesus, instinctively I turned to Msgr. de Ségur, and there I found myself in an atmosphere like heaven. I cannot say it better; it was only there that I understood Jesus.

Without analyzing what I was feeling in the depths of my heart, without trying to establish the difference between a good confessor and a true spiritual director, I realized only that the former imposed his will on me, and the latter made me love what he asked of me. In the former, I found a master, in the latter a father. The influence of a true director was essential in my youth. It must have continued by the grace of God until the present time.

That was the first call I received from the Lord to the special vocation of director of souls.[86]

The influence of Fr. de Ségur was evident also in a letter to his parents, written by Henri Chaumont from the seminary at Versailles. As his spiritual director had advised, he put Jesus at the center of his faith:

I wanted it so much, this happiness that so many people search for in vain. I found what the whole world could not give me. I found Jesus! All those dreams of happiness that humans take pleasure in nourishing in their hearts faded away. I had found Jesus, and my heart wanted only to love more fully each day and to make God's glory known to the world.[87]

Msgr. de Ségur was equally sure of the young man's vocation: he said to Henri's mother, "Your son will be a priest." In the following years he remained attentive to his future, intervening so that he would be enrolled at Saint Sulpice and recommending that Msgr. Grandvaux be his spiritual advisor. Msgr. de Ségur presided over the formation of The White Oak Society, whose members resolved to remain detached from material goods all through their careers in the Church. As assistant at Saint Marcel, Henri placed himself directly under the guidance of Fr. de Ségur, whom he saw every week, and who asked him to accompany the spiritual journeys of several women of high society, specifically Mme de Tury. It was with him that Fr. Chaumont deepened his understanding of the writings

---

[86] Quoted by Msgr. Debout.
[87] Letter to his father, June 1855, quoted by Msgr. Debout.

of Francis de Sales. It was probably to Msgr. de Ségur that he first confided his project to organize a group of women who would assist him in the spiritual conversations at Saint Marcel (see Chapter V) and who encouraged him in the undertaking.

From this time on, Fr. Chaumont joined Msgr. de Ségur in the effort to encourage frequent Communion. Following his influence, the young assistant was able to have the clergy of his parish placed under the patronage of St. Francis de Sales. Unfortunately, Fr. Chaumont was not able to be present at the ceremony, celebrated January 25, 1868, by Fr. Lagarde, the vicar general, due to an attack of rheumatism, complicated by cerebral fever so severe as to endanger his life.[88] Msgr. de Ségur, who visited his disciple every day, made him promise that if he survived, he would make a pilgrimage to Annecy, to the tomb of his true spiritual master:

You must not die so soon, my child. Since men are not able to save you, promise to the Saint that you have loved so dearly to go to thank him at his glorious tomb, at Annecy, if he can win your healing.[89]

In June of that same year Fr. Chaumont fulfilled his promise. He agreed with Msgr. de Ségur to stop en route to consult with Mother Mary de Sales Chappuis, at the Visitation in Troyes and Msgr. Mermillod,

---

[88] Msgr. Laveille saw in this illness the fulfilment of the wish made by Msgr. de Ségur for the New Year: "I wish for you, my dear friend, as many crosses as you can carry this year, with the help of God's grace.
[89] Quoted by Msgr. Laveille.

Bishop of Geneva and Annecy. These two were interested in a project similar to his, to found a society of Christian women. (See Chapter V.)[90] Shortly after his return, he gave the publisher the first of his spiritual lessons, taken from the works of St. Francis de Sales, *Treatise on Temptations,* for which Msgr. de Ségur wrote a preface presenting the collected articles of *Spiritual Direction.*

With generous devotion, the author has collected and organized what comes from the pen of St. Francis de Sales concerning Christian virtue and more specifically what concerns the sanctification and the direction of souls. Thank God, the treasure was so abundant that, in most cases there was more material than was necessary to compose a treatise, as complete as if the blessed bishop had composed it himself.

We can see that more and more the daily activities of the assistant at Sainte Clotilde resembled those of Msgr. de Ségur even though the people who flocked to Chaumont's confessional were a more varied group, and included more women. He adhered to what Msgr. de Ségur had written about Christian renunciation and used it himself in spiritual guidance, even in counselling his mother: The saints "found so much in God that they had found everything, and having found it, how could they waste time regretting what was

---

[90] Bringing a letter from Msgr. de Ségur, Fr. Chaumont was able to obtain an audience with these two prestigious people to whom he wanted to explain his project and whose responses he would receive.

nothing: themselves. . . . Rather than bringing sadness, renunciation gives us the only real consolation." [91]

Following this precept, biographies of Fr. Chaumont show him imposing sacrifices on himself in order to help a soul who was risking damnation, substituting his own acts of piety to compensate for the other's wrongs. Msgr. de Ségur had given him the example:

It is certain that the blind priest was not satisfied with giving his spiritual children his time, his strength, and all the resources of his heart and mind. Rather he "paid" ceaselessly for them: For years he imposed harsh penances on himself in reparation for sacrileges committed by some young people. . . . His disciple, Fr. Chaumont, who also planned to become a spiritual director, was fearful, "knowing at what price (Fr. de Ségur) had won so many souls to Jesus Christ." (M. de Hédouville)

Fr. Chaumont always found moral support in Msgr. de Ségur. The latter advised one of his nieces, Mlle de Mallaret, to join the group of Daughters of St. Francis de Sales. In the same spirit he encouraged Fr. Gabiller to collaborate with Fr. Chaumont in the work of St. Benedict Labre for the alumni of the Christian Brothers, who wanted to further the work of the Gospel in the world. He encouraged Fr. Chaumont to create a group of priests formed in the spirituality of St. Francis de Sales who could give their support to his

---

[91]Letter written September 11, 1872, and quoted by Monseigneur Laveille. Fr. Chaumont is referring here to Msgr. de Ségur's *Treatise on Piety and the Interior Life,* which had just been published.

Daughters. His answer was clear: "There is no doubt; the good Lord wants it. It is time to start a first group." [92] The original rule for the group mentions Msgr. de Ségur as director. [93] Even as he was nearing death, [94] Msgr. de Ségur's interest in Fr. Chaumont's Salesian works did not lessen, as Msgr. Laveille reported:

On January 29, 1880, he came to celebrate the feast of St. Francis de Sales at the little sanctuary on the avenue de Breteuil. At the end of the ceremony he said to Fr. Chaumont, "How I love this dear family! Here we are fully in the presence of Jesus' love. The soul is at ease and joyfully free of the banal formulas of piety." A little later he added, "I left the 'House of the Good God' and my conversations with the company there, especially the good and saintly Mme Carré, feeling as if I had absorbed a perfume of joy and peace. (Msgr. Laveille)

Henri Chaumont had always considered Msgr. de Ségur his spiritual director, [95] but it was he who accompanied the prelate in his last days. He said to the priests of St. Francis de Sales:

---

[92] Quoted by Msgr. Laveille.

[93] Fr. Chaumont did not have confidence in his ability to direct a group of priests. He asked Msgr. de Ségur to accept that responsibility. But the prelate's time was already too limited, so in fact Fr. Chaumont accepted the position.

[94] He died June 9, 1881.

[95] "This priest who insisted on the docility of the spiritual director was, on his part, equally accepting when seeking spiritual guidance. He never made a decision of any importance without discussing it with Msgr. de Ségur. The three Salesian societies were the work of both priests." (Msgr. Laveille)

Everyone who knew him, and everyone could not be wrong, recognized that his greatest virtue was the love of God and love of his fellows. It is impossible to say how intimately he lived with God; this love was not only fervent but it was also affectionate and had become a passion. It was only natural that the love of God was the driving force in his life, the inspiration for all his thoughts and words. This love was a lively emotion but also a learned theology. With time, this inner flame became brighter, to the point that we can only say that it is impossible to love God more completely than he.

Nevertheless, there was something even more remarkable in this passionate heart: his love for others. Great love when he found himself face to face with a soul. And who could say what he was able to inspire in young people with the love that he offered. It is not enough to offer charity; we have to really love, if we want to do God's work. In spite of the freedom that his love for others provided him, no one ever had the least familiarity with him. And that was the necessary condition for the success of his ministry.[96]

Anatole de Ségur, the brother of the late priest, asked Fr. Chaumont to write a supplement to the biography that he had prepared[97] in order to express the spiritual message of his brother's life. On January 7, 1892, Fr. Chaumont gave the archbishop of Paris, Cardinal

---

[96] Talk given to a meeting of the Priests of St. Francis de Sales, June 13, 1881, quoted by Msgr. Debout.

[97] *Memoirs of a Brother,* 1882.

Richard, a dossier composed with the purpose of opening a process of beatification for Msgr. de Ségur.

CHAPTER V

FIRST ATTEMPTS TO START A SALESIAN SOCIETY FOR WOMEN

The pastoral duties confided to an assistant at Saint Marcel were necessarily very diverse; nevertheless, it began gradually to be concentrated around the work of confession and spiritual direction. Msgr. de Ségur, who had observed the particular aptitudes of the young priest, encouraged this orientation. Fr. Chaumont wanted to strengthen the faith of the women who looked to him for guidance, and turn that faith toward participation in evangelization within the framework of the Church. He placed the new society under the patronage of the bishop of Annecy and Geneva.

Assistant at Saint Marcel

Fr. Chaumont also developed a program of catechism using the parish buildings especially for the poor residing in that area and thought of combining this project with the formation of an elite group, among the Christian women, who would assist him. Msgr. Laveille explained it in these words:

The little boarding school directed by the Misses de la Motte accepted with enthusiasm the spiritual support of the young priest. While teaching classes in religious education in the school, he had noticed several young girls who might welcome the opportunity for serious formation. In the parish, among the women who regularly attended daily Mass, there were many who were drawn to living "the perfect life." The young priest decided to bring together these two groups of kindred souls, united in their commitment, so that they could be strengthened beyond their personal faith. A homogeneous group, if he could in fact bring it together, meeting regularly would allow him to give special instruction concerning spiritual progress at a higher level than he could preach to the large group of parishioners at Sunday masses.

He planned to organize this little group into an association and prepared a rule taken from the writings of St. Francis de Sales:

As I am imagining it, the first six months [of participation in the association] would be devoted principally to study of the rule and how practicing this rule might change one's life; the other six months would be, on the contrary, finding out concretely the results of living these principles. At the end of a year, the promises (without being obligatory in themselves) would include the religious virtues and also the specific ones recommended by the rule. An act of consecration, explicit and irreversible, will be written then by each member and given to each one's spiritual director.[98]

A first obstacle seemed to present itself, but it was apparently avoided: What if the spiritual director of the person being considered was not in favor of the project of association? Fr. Chaumont took the initiative in speaking to about twenty young girls from

---

[98] Letter from Fr. Chaumont, December 11, 1867, in *Spiritual Letters*.

the parish. He asked Mlle Honorine Nicolas to lead them. At the beginning, there was a certain enthusiasm for this group in the parish. Fr. Chaumont did not let this first emotion mislead him; he reminded Miss Loiseau, who was under his guidance, that it is prudent not to be deceived by a first reaction but to remain steadfast in one's own practices.

It is marvellous, my child, to see how this little association already delights the Heart of our Lord, and answers the desires of some souls. But keep in mind the reality of this work, a very small and fragile beginning, so vulnerable that a little pride or ambition could destroy it. . . . Oh, but if this little association of humble souls does some good, if these souls remain constant in their humility and their nothingness, finding their happiness in making amends for thousands and thousands of past failings by a life as perfect as possible.[99]

Fr. Chaumont was right to be cautious: After several months, rivalries began to divide the young girls, and the group separated. Only a small core, centred on Mlle Loiseau, remained. The priest made another attempt with another group of young girls from a secular professional school, near the church of Saint Lambert de Vaugirard, directed by Mlle Saint-André. The director, several of her colleagues, and two of the students adopted the rule that he proposed. Unfortunately, once again there were conflicts of

---

[99] Letter to Miss Loiseau, December 1867, in *Spiritual Letters*. It is interesting to note the importance of the notion of reparation, so much a part of devotion to the Sacred Heart.

influence that caused divisions, and the priest thought it wise to withdraw from the project.

First Pilgrimage to Annecy

All was not lost, however. Msgr. de Ségur suggested that Fr. Chaumont, who was preparing his pilgrimage to Annecy,[100] meet Mother Marie de Sales Chappuis and Msgr. Gaspard Mermillod, who had both undertaken similar ventures. At Troyes, Fr. Louis Brisson, chaplain of the Visitation, with the help of the superior, Mother de Sales, had recruited some former students from the boarding school run by the sisters. He asked them to organize support for young girls, and to counter the difficulties that had surfaced in previous attempts, discord and loss of commitment, he thought of forming a community living in the daily world but nourished by Salesian spirituality. Like Msgr. de Ségur, Msgr. Mermillod, bishop of Geneva, encouraged the project; his goal was to establish religious life in the city of Calvin, even though he knew that the local government would set up obstacles to the presence of a true Catholic congregation.

The first profession of the Oblates of St. Francis de Sales took place in the autumn of 1871 with Msgr. de Ségur presiding. Fr. Chaumont arrived at Troyes at the time of this installation (June 1868). Fr. Brisson asked him to join this project, but Mother Chappuis was

---

[100] This pilgrimage was in thanksgiving to St. Francis de Sales for healing from the sickness he suffered in January 1868, from which he nearly died.

more prudent: "Let the others continue, but you found your own society as the good Lord tells you." [101]

After eight days of excursions in Switzerland, the pilgrim met Msgr. Gaspard Mermillod (1824–1896)[102] in Geneva. The bishop gave Chaumont enthusiastic approval for the project and the rule he had developed. But Fr. Chaumont continued to Annecy, to the chapel of the Visitation where the relics of St. Francis de Sales and Ste. Jeanne de Chantal are enshrined.[103] He brought his project for the association before these two holy ones.

At 6:00 in the morning, I celebrate the holy Mass on the tomb of St. Francis de Sales. When I have finished giving thanks, and when I have prayed in a special way

---

[101] Quoted by Monseigneur Laveille.

[102] He was a bishop in constant combat for the faith. As a priest at Notre Dame in Geneva, he was named auxiliary bishop of Lausanne, residing in Geneva, which drew the hostility of the local authorities. In 1873 he was expelled from Swiss territory. He began an important career as a preacher in France. He was very familiar with the parish of Sainte Clotilde, where he preached the Lenten offices in 1862. He returned to preach the sermons of charity in favor of the poor in Ireland in May 1862 and April 20, 1863, for the benefit of the poor and ill in Poland. In an address on February 23, 1868, concerning the Church and the condition of the working class, he recalled the responsibilities of the upper classes on "the dreadful and dangerous question of the situation of the working poor." On April 14, 1872, evoking the lessons of the Commune, he denounced the peril arising from the elimination of God from the social order.

[103] This was the church of St. Francis in the old part of Annecy. The modern basilica on the hills overlooking the lake was built in 1930. The remains of the two saints were transferred there.

for everyone, and especially for those to whom I most owe my gratitude, I begin my day. That means to return as often as possible and as long as possible to the little chapel of the Visitation. When I am not there, I am—in body but not in soul or in spirit—on the shores of Lake Annecy or in my little room, wherever I may be, I am at the feet of St. Francis de Sales and Ste. Jeanne de Chantal, and I keep watch over everyone who passes, committing them to our two great saints. If there is a need, people tell me what it is, and I write it down. The tasks and the people go by, that's all. I walk for a bit, visiting the places that mark memories of the saints in Annecy, and all is well.[104]

Msgr. Laveille summed up the fruits of the pilgrimage:

His project became more clear: Explain as much as possible to women of the upper classes who have a strong faith the rules for the "perfect life" set down by St. Francis de Sales, publish the code of recommendations for daily living, short and simple, taken from The Introduction to the Devout Life; bring to the people who might adopt this rule the encouragement and the support of a spiritual family; create a sort of institution without vows in the midst of worldly society, including even married women. Such was the plan he adopted at the end of eight days spent almost without interruption in the sanctuary he loved so well.

---

[104] Unpublished letter dated June 13, 1868, quoted by Msgr. Laveille

For the time being, nothing more could be done, because Fr. Chaumont left Saint Marcel for Sainte Clotilde.

Madame Carré de Malberg

In June 1869, Fr. Chaumont and Mme Carré de Malberg met for the first time. Caroline Barbe Colchen was born in 1829 in Metz, in the region of Lorraine, in eastern France. She married her first cousin, Paul Carré de Malberg, at the age of twenty. He was a young military officer at the time.[105] When Mme Carré met Fr. Chaumont, her husband was a commander stationed in Paris. They had four children, but only one survived, Paul Jr. Msgr. Laveille described the first meeting:

Sustained by her union with God, Mme. Carré, had dealt courageously with her suffering, and her salon in rue Martignac had become a meeting place for the elegant society of a wealthy area of Paris near les Invalides. Everyone appreciated her graciousness, her generosity toward all in distress, and especially her capacity to answer discreetly and perceptively to the most intimate confidences entrusted to her. Ever since her arrival in Paris she had been looking for a spiritual director. Some of her friends had mentioned the young assistant at Sainte Clotilde, to whom so

---

[105] In his biography of Carré de Malberg, Msgr. Laveille did not avoid discussing the difficulties apparent from the very beginning of the marriage, caused by the abruptness of the young officer and his lack of concern for his wife. She, on the other hand, tried to understand her husband and bring him happiness.

many looked for direction. But the priest's rather distant, somewhat cold manner had kept her away. She needed the encouragement of Miss Pauline Girard, a friend of the family, before she could approach this frightening confessional.

After giving absolution, Fr. Chaumont asked her about her life. She had just lost a beautiful little girl, returned to God at the age of only four; she spoke to Fr. Chaumont about her grief and her distress.

"Poor child," he responded and found eloquent words of hope for her. As he spoke, Mme Carré understood that even in the midst of such loss and pain, she could find inward happiness, if she could ask for a close relationship with the Lord. Not having had adequate spiritual direction, she had begun to succumb to sadness. The supernatural life with its different degrees, its conditions, its difficulties, its merits, its ultimate glorious triumph in the next life, such were the horizons that her faith and her will were to open for her.

She still hesitated, but, encouraged by her brother, Fr. Colchen, a Dominican, she accepted the direction of Fr. Chaumont, who was nine years younger than her. The priest quickly had the intuition that Mme Carré was the person God had chosen to establish the association he was planning. He asked her to put into practice the methods proposed by St. Francis de Sales to begin serious progress toward sainthood: confession and a six-day retreat.

He explained the rule for the life of devotion to Mme Carré and to a few women of strong faith who attended her salon. He encouraged her to begin some more intimate meetings for people like herself who sought perfection in fulfilling their duties within the family and in social relationships.

Soon an elite group was formed among Mme Carré's friends. The priest was received separately, at times that would not trouble the intimacy of the meeting. The reputation of each person was strictly respected and all worldly conversation was excluded. They often prayed together and encouraged each other to accept cheerfully the difficulties they experienced and the inevitable self-denial that ensues when a woman must choose between God and a worldly life. Fr. Chaumont was always consulted; he helped to clarify their projects, spoke the voice of reason to those carried away by their imagination or whose activities departed from their purpose, and drew all their hearts toward the magnificent goal of holiness through fulfilling their roles as wives and mothers. The salon, filled with the sweetness of the Gospel, could become a hearthside glowing at the center of Paris to warm all those in its reach. (Msgr. Laveille)

This activity on the part of Mme Carré embodied the very heart of what St. Francis de Sales called for in the *Introduction to the Devout Life:* The quest for a holy life does not require withdrawing from the world, something impossible for people who have a certain position in society, like Mme Carré. As the wife of an officer, she was obliged to maintain a level of social life, dictated by his rank. But she brought her ideals to this worldly life, with the help of Fr. Chaumont. Hers was a Christian *salon,* modeled, so to speak, on Mme

Swetchine's and hoping to serve as an example to others.

Spiritual Progress

The Church was in the midst of the discussion of the infallibility of the pope, in preparation for the next Vatican Council. The debate overflowed into the newspapers and Paris *salons*. Fr. Chaumont had to advise those under his spiritual direction to remain completely outside of the question, only asking that they maintain their total obedience to the pope. At the same time he decided to publish a sequel to *The Treatise on Temptations,* drawn from the collection of *Spiritual Direction of Saint Francis de Sales,* entitled *A Treatise on Friendship* with a preface by Msgr. Mermillod. *A Treatise on Humility* followed shortly after.

During the Franco-Prussian War (1870–1871), as we have seen, Fr. Chaumont was obliged to leave Paris. Nevertheless, he maintained his relationships with those under his spiritual direction, among them Mme Carré, who had found refuge in the region of Toulouse. Director Chaumont was sometimes harsh with her, reminding her of the importance of humility, and of avoiding self-pity in spite of her situation. Indeed, she took advantage of this exile in the countryside, far from the life of Paris, to develop her own practices of piety.

She left the chateau where she was residing only for her daily walk in the park with her friend Mme de Saint-Jean. She spent the rest of her time in the chapel, where she could always find the company of our

Savior, or in the study, where she helped her young son with his studies. She soon adopted the habit of reciting the rosary and the Office of the Holy Virgin. The theme of this office was wonderfully close to the counsel given to her by Fr. Chaumont. (Msgr. Laveille)

Fr. Chaumont's letters continued to encourage her spiritual life:

What are you doing, my child, for our dear France? What are you doing for our dear Rome? What are you doing for the beloved bride of Jesus, the Church? All this simply means, how are you giving of yourself to these noble and holy causes, how are you using the many graces that our Lord offers you, and the ingenious resources of devotion? You receive so much, my daughter: what do you give back to God? With what enthusiasm, with what generosity?[106]

For these elite souls of the nineteenth century, Msgr. de Ségur, Fr. Chaumont, or the faithful whose spiritual life they directed, certain behaviors were perfectly normal and unquestioned, but they may seem shocking to the twenty-first-century reader: to inflict penances on oneself by substitution, or using the instruments of mortification, Fr. Chaumont cautions that they be used with discretion, but he does not forbid them:

He was fully convinced that if one wishes to save souls and especially bind them closely to Jesus our savior, it was necessary to suffer for them and teach them

---

[106] Letter of Fr. Chaumont to Mme Carré, April 1, 1871, quoted by Msgr. Laveille.

penitence. It was not enough for him to spend days in the confessional and to devote a part of his nights to writing letters to those entrusted to him, fighting sleep by the most heroic methods: he willingly used the instruments of penitence. Sometimes carried away with ardor in his speeches, he revealed to his listeners the iron bracelets he wore around his arms. If his own zeal encountered a soul too blind or too obstinate to recognize God, he imposed further sufferings on himself, in order to "do violence to God."[107]

Without hesitation he advised regular practices of mortification but cautioned against any abuse. (Msgr. Laveille)[108]

Beyond the quest for personal sanctification through observing the rules of St. Francis de Sales, Fr. Chaumont was thinking of organizing a society of Christian women from the upper classes who could evangelize and perform works of charity. He introduced Mme Carré and two other women whom he counseled, seeing in them the nucleus of this future society. He asked them to make a commitment to serve only God in the ways proposed by St. Francis de

---

[107] This expression, which seems quite strange to us today, meant to the priest the desire to "save souls" and to oblige God, in a way, to intervene to lead them away from their sinful lives and to conversion. The holy priest of Ars inflicted such penances on himself for a similar reason.

[108] The author quotes here a letter from Fr. Chaumont dated September 20, 1872. It urged moderation in acts of mortification, certainly intended not to impinge on the freedom of those he directed but also not to alarm the husbands of these women who would see an exaggerated piety in such measures.

Sales.[109] Mme Carré quickly brought two new souls to this group, Mlle Stiltz and Mlle de Parieu, the daughter of a former minister and president of the Council of State. In August 1872, Mmes Carré and Maure and Mlle Stiltz went to Luhon with Fr. Colchen, who made this meeting a sort of retreat through which to initiate them, quite rigorously, to practicing the teachings of the Gospels.

Following the Dominican priest's orders, the wife of Colonel Carré could be seen carrying a big wicker basket of provisions to a poor woman; he also entrusted to her care a woman covered with purulent sores. For weeks this woman of elegant society knelt beside the half-decomposed body, to calm its burning pain as best she could. And as if such experiences were not enough to break her pride, the vigilant priest pretended for a long time not to be attentive to the needs of Mme Carré's soul while he gave ready counsel and direction to her two companions. (Msgr. Laveille)

It is clear in this description that Fr. Colchen, as well as Fr. Chaumont, seeing in Mme Carré an elite soul, led her down a more difficult path toward humility, realizing that she would bear it and be strengthened, something that many would not have been able to do.

Second Pilgrimage to Annecy and Decisive Steps

---

[109] The reference here is to *An Authentic Declaration to Impress on the Soul Its Resolution to Serve God and to Conclude the Acts of Penance*, St. Francis de Sales, *Introduction to the Devout Life*, Part I, Ch. XX, Ryan translation.

Feeling the need for rest, Fr. Chaumont decided in September 1872 to make a second pilgrimage to Annecy. For the second time also, he passed through Troyes in order to consult Mother Chappuis, who continued to encourage him in his project. He stayed at the same hotel in Geneva, trying to find peace and serenity again.

I am living here a little like a hermit, praying frequently when I can, writing a great deal and taking walks when it is God's will. Were it not for my nerves, which have been sick for a long time, I would be perfectly well. But the Lord has showed me that for the time being he won't give me further healing; it would be a wilful illusion to believe that I will soon find relief. Then let his loving will be done in us, around us, in this world, in the next. Let him do with us and with everything what he wants.[110]

He wrote these impressions to Mme Carré and suggested that she also give herself completely to God's will:

We were led into a modest room, where the Saint counseled his dear daughters and brought about so many wonderful things. The narrowness, the simplicity of this room touched me deeply. I had to turn aside to hide my emotion from the others who were present. I prayed for some special souls, you, my child, your friend whose faith is so strong, and some others.

You understand the true meaning of what I write: The good Lord has placed both of you in a saintly vocation,

---

[110] Letter from Fr. Chaumont in *Spiritual Letters.*

in which you should wish to continue, fulfilling your duties with nobility and constancy. Let nothing lead you to neglect your obligations. At the same time, God seems to be at work, drawing your souls particularly near to him. What is he asking of you? I can't resolve the question, and the Lord seems to want to remain silent for a while on the subject. Sometimes I think he has infinitely merciful plans for you, but you may be the instruments of a very different plan, one that I can't foresee, but that you yourselves sometimes seem to glimpse.[111]

But things suddenly began to happen very rapidly, and a confluence of circumstances made it possible for Mme Carré and Mme Maure to go to Annecy while Fr. Chaumont was still there. It seems that the pilgrimage of the little group to the Gallery, the house where the Visitation was founded, cast an unexpected light on the mission they sought.

Having received Communion from the hand of their spiritual father at the altar of St. Francis de Sales, in the monastery of the Visitation, the two women visited the Gallery with him and saw the modest room, four square meters, which had been the chapel of the illustrious Motherhouse of the Visitation of Holy Mary. What special graces fell from the heart of Jesus at that moment into their souls? We have no way of knowing. But we do know that as they left the Gallery, the resolution was made to begin a Work, under the patronage of St. Francis de Sales, intended to prepare a few souls of fervent faith, living in the midst of the

---

[111] Chaumont, Henri: *La Premiére Mére de la Societé des Filles de Saint François de Sales,* Centre Salesien, Paris, 1894.

world, and able to bear valiantly the sweet and gentle yoke of our Savior Jesus, to make him loved by all around them through the humble means that they possessed.

The spiritual father suggested an experimental rule for this first society. They agreed to meet in Paris for the first time, on October 15, [1872,] the feast of Ste. Teresa of Avila.

The pilgrims separated, their souls filled with joy but also astonished and fearful as they recognized the importance of what they had just done. But grace, which had inspired everything, brought peace as well, and with this peace the father blessed his daughters. They in turn promised to give all of their generosity and devotion to the newly born Work.[112]

Fr. Chaumont felt that he had just received a special insight for the direction of his mission:

Many years later, remembering that second pilgrimage to Annecy, he declared that from that moment on he saw the Society of Priests and that of the Daughters spreading the gospel throughout the world exactly as it would come to pass. He no longer doubted the success of this mission. (Msgr. Debout)

---

[112] Chaumont, H. *La Premiere Mere.*

CHAPTER VI

DAUGHTERS AND SONS
OF SAINT FRANCIS DE SALES

The Societies of the Sons and Daughters of St. Francis de Sales were the result of the work of Fr. Chaumont and the extraordinary soul Mme Carré de Malberg, who put herself under his spiritual guidance at Sainte Clotilde. Their project took shape during the second pilgrimage to Annecy in the autumn of 1872. Fr. Chaumont was acting on the intuition of St. Francis de Sales when he proposed to a group of women with a strong Catholic faith to unite in evangelizing activities in service of the Church. Nevertheless, this kind of life seemed relatively new in the nineteenth century when it was difficult to see beyond a dichotomy between the laity and the religious life; several years' experience were necessary before the originality of the idea could be fully appreciated.

The Beginning

On October 15, 1872, Fr. Chaumont met with the administrator of the orphanage of the Holy Childhood of Mary, Mlle Justine Korsten, the priest's aunt and godmother, and Mme Carré, Mme Sallard and Mme Maure. They gathered in the offices of social services at Saint Sulpice.

As soon as they arrived, the priest and his spiritual daughters recited the "Veni Sancte Spiritus," a "Hail

Mary," and an invocation to St. Francis de Sales and Ste. Jeanne de Chantal. He then read a few pages titled "The Rule of the Daughters of St. Francis de Sales," which he had sketched out at Annecy. The founder set forth in a few articles an entire plan for a life inspired by the Gospel; he was not afraid to propose the life of the first Christians as an ideal.[113] He indicated as a code of perfection the holy Scriptures studied in the light of the writings of St. Francis de Sales, placing his associates under the patronage of the saintly bishop and Ste. Jeanne de Chantal, asking from them a special zeal for the sanctification of souls. He ended with a chapter concerning their relationship to one another.

This last unfinished chapter became immediately the object of some deliberation. They came to the decision that the three women would meet once a week to hear an exhortation by their spiritual director. They would take turns leading the meetings, and at each meeting the leader would take the title and the authority of "spiritual mother," and she would impose penances for infractions to the rule. (Msgr. Laveille)

Fr. Chaumont himself also left a brief testimony to this scene:

"The spiritual father explained in general terms the thought behind the project that was taking shape

---

[113] One thinks here of the *Acts of the Apostles:* "The multitude of believers had only one heart and one soul. No one claimed anything as his or her own but among them all was held in common. The apostles witnessed powerfully to the Resurrection of the Lord Jesus and all were greatly respected." (Acts, IV, 12)

*under the protection of St. Teresa of Avila, whose feast
day they were celebrating. He spoke especially of the
goal of living a Christian and Evangelical life in the
midst of the world, as described by St. Francis de Sales
in his Introduction to the Devout Life and then of the
need to give wise counsel and examples of good
conduct whenever opportunities would present
themselves.*[114]

The meeting ended as each one recognized her faults
before the others present.[115] The following week a
fourth woman also under the spiritual guidance of Fr.
Chaumont came to join the original three: Mlle Bot.
The priest asked that they maintain absolute discretion
regarding the existence of the group and requested that
they never use the religious names they had chosen
outside of their meetings: sister Jeanne de Chantal for
Mme Carré, sister Theresa of Jesus for Mme Maure,
sister Marie-Madeleine for Mme Sallard. In fact,
addressing each other as *sister* expressed the close
community among them. The choice of religious
names is more ambiguous. Surely their intention was
to place themselves under the patronage of a saint, but
it could also be a mark of their wish to be religious
sisters in a worldly society. We recall that Salesian
spirituality never asks that one abandon the condition

---

[114] Chaumont, *La Premiére Mére*.

[115] This practice, which may seem surprising, is an imitation of
the life of religious sisters, where the members of a community
recognize among themselves their actions that have been
contrary to the Rule. It is not a public confession since it is not
intended to reveal sins but rather failures along the way to
perfection. Fr. Chaumont was quick to limit excesses in the zeal
of the first Daughters of St. Francis de Sales.

of a layperson, the more so since some of the women were married.

The meetings were first held on Tuesday, but because of Fr. Chaumont's duties in the parish, they were moved to Friday. They always began with the reading of the minutes of the last meeting. Then the spiritual father gave the floor to one of his daughters, who discussed a question of faith and faithful living.[116] Then came the telling of their failures to observe the Rule.[117] There was a tendency to extend this examination of conduct to a confession of sins; it was necessary to maintain the strict limits of the practice. Clarifying the Rule, a discussion of possible future members of the group and an exhortation by Fr. Chaumont brought the meeting to an end. The first candidates had been selected by Fr. Chaumont himself, but after several weeks, the priest wanted the Daughters themselves to discuss new members.

At each meeting, one of the women served as spiritual mother or president; another transcribed the priest's words and read them as collected at the previous session; a third had the modest role of "servant," helping with the small needs of her sisters. From the beginning, Mme Carré was elected spiritual mother for a month; Mme Sallard was given the duties of

---

[116] This is an important point: normally one would expect that Fr. Chaumont himself would take this role.

[117] This restriction maintains the distinction between the inner and the outer self. Inner faults are a matter for confession; outer are questions of conduct. The Rule aims at guiding the spiritual life beyond what is normally expected of a Christian.

secretary; Mme Maure was the "servant." (Msgr. Laveille)

On January 3, 1873, the group met at the apartment of Msgr. de Ségur, at his request. He spoke to the members, now thirteen in number, of the importance of making frequent Confession and daily Communion. Mlle de Parieu, Mlle Stiltz, and Mlle J..... pronounced their consecration. Msgr. de Ségur was so charmed by the faith of these women that he blessed them effusively and declared to Fr. Chaumont a week later, "What a perfume these souls left for me. The house is still sweetly scented." The founder wrote, "Msgr. de Ségur is officially nothing for our group but in fact he is everything. He is continually blessing my daughters and encouraging them through the person of their humble spiritual father." [118]

To mark this very special day, the new association decided to put a plaque of thanksgiving in the chapel of the prelate, a silver heart enclosing the names of the first Daughters of St. Francis de Sales. (Msgr. Laveille)

At first the group met in small quarters, the rue de la Cassette, near the Luxembourg Gardens; then they moved to the parlor of the Convent of the Soeurs de la Retraite. There was more space there, but their presence awakened curiosity and commentaries, some of them unpleasant. Fr. Brisson, founder of the Oblates of St. Francis de Sales, offered the use of an apartment he rented in Paris (79, rue de Vaugirard). This solution

---

[118] Letter from H. Chaumont (Paris, February 14, 1873) in *Lettres Spirituelles.*

helped to stop the suspicions that weighed on the Association, but ambiguities remained. Fr. Brisson was thinking of eventually integrating the Parisian group with his own. But Mother Marie de Sales Chappuis, considered nearly an oracle by the two priests, did not approve. She said to Fr. Chaumont:

"I very much respect Fr. Brisson and he is right to look for support in the work he does. I pray God for his success. But don't ally yourself with him; he must have his oblates and you your daughters of St. Francis de Sales.[119]

The House of the Good God

The first three women elected Mme Carré "Superior" for a year on October 8, 1873. Mme Carré, Mme Sallard, and Mme Maure formed a personal council around Fr. Chaumont. This was the embryo of the General Council of the Society. After leaving the refuge provided by Fr. Brisson, the associates rented a little apartment at 21 rue Vaneau, behind les Invalides. One of the Daughters, Mlle Poussardieu, went to live there, and to avoid any rumors or misinterpretations, the group took on the appearance of women engaged in charitable works, preparing dressings for the sick, with the name of "The Charitable Workshop of Saint Veronica." Nevertheless, more problems came to light in the form of meddling. Due to frictions between Mlle Pousssardieu and Mlle Bot, the former was sent by the Council to the diocese of Nancy. There, with the help

---

[119] H. Chaumont, *Notes et Souvenirs.*

of the priest of Bréménil, her native village, she formed a little group attached to the Parisian center.

Mme Carré, after another brief stay at the Visitation along with Mme Maure, understood that the group needed to be more autonomous. The Council decided to rent a small private house, 31 avenue Breteuil, once again near les Invalides. Mlle Bot and Mlle Stiltz went to live there. Mme Sallard found a name for it: the "House of the Good God."[120] This happened in May 1874. There were twenty-five Daughters of St. Francis de Sales. At the end of that year, the number had doubled; they were fifty-two, about fifteen of whom had made their profession.[121] One of the rooms in the House of the Good God became the meeting room for the Society of Christian Women;[122] another was made into a chapel.

In the final months of 1875, the new coadjutor of Paris asked Msgr. Richard,[123] with the agreement of Fr.

---

[120] She declared, "What could you be doing in this house, except the holy work leading to the glory of God? So whose house can it be? It belongs truly and principally to God. The only Master of this house is God; we don´t need to look any further for a name that is so obvious. The name is "the House of the Good God."

[121] Here again we find a religious term, but it refers only to a commitment within the group, as Fr. Chaumont explained in the first Rule. (Chapter V)

[122] See below.

[123] Msgr. Richard de la Vergne (1819–1908) was bishop of Belley in 1871; in 1875 he became coadjutor of Cardinal Guibert, archbishop of Paris. He succeeded him in 1886 and was made a cardinal three months later.

d'Hulst, to intercede with Cardinal Guibert[124] for permission to celebrate Mass in "the House of the Good God." The archbishop resisted for some time but ultimately granted not only this request but also the privilege of keeping the Real Presence in their meeting room. Honored in this way, the oratory became the Chapel of the Daughters of St. Francis de Sales.

On December 9, 1875, Fr. d'Hulst, who had recently been named prosecutor[125] for the diocese, came in the name of Cardinal Guibert to celebrate Mass in the house of the Daughters, and place the Blessed Sacrament there. The Christian Women filled the chapel, and many Daughters of St. Francis de Sales were among those present. Fr. d'Hulst, who recognized them, made frequent and quite transparent allusions to them in his talk, giving them comfort and hope. (Msgr. Laveille)

One of the women under Fr. Chaumont's spiritual guidance, Marie Augustine Rousselet, who had entered the Society of the Daughters at a very young age, took over the direction of the House of the Good God (March 25, 1875).

The house very quickly became too small for all its uses. In spite of an emotional attachment to the previous house, in 1889 the women moved to 50 rue de Bourgogne, still near les Invalides. It was a

---

[124] Msgr. Hyppolyte Guibert (1802–1886), bishop of Viviers (1842), archbishop of Tours (1857) became archbishop of Paris in 1871, to succeed Msgr. Darboy. He became a cardinal in 1873.
[125] "Promoteur de justice," prosecutor for the Church in ecclesiastical tribunals, defends the rights of the Church.

beautiful house with some rooms still retaining their gold decoration and big enough to accommodate the services offered by the House of the Good God. There was also sufficient room for the offices of the Work of Mary Immaculate and the Christian Teachers.

Madame Carré Leaves Paris

On April 14, 1874, Colonel Carré was named assistant chief of staff to the general headquarters of the third army in residence in Rouen. As a result, Mme Carré who had been, with Fr. Chaumont, the mainstay of the creation of the Daughters of St. Francis de Sales, had to leave the founder. Before she left, she gave a new role to Mlle Stiltz.

The qualities of mind and heart of the young associate (Mlle Stiltz) and her perfect understanding of Fr. Chaumont's views had guided her choice. Nevertheless, she had to introduce Mlle Stiltz to the principles of spiritual government. Mme Carré came to live at the House of the Good God for the month before her departure, making a sort of retreat, in order to give the two associates who were living there an example of perfect discipline, and especially to show Mlle Stiltz the essence of her future responsibilities: the need for self-sacrifice and for spiritual wisdom, found not in human intelligence and experience, but in the teachings of the Gospels. The sublime beauty of evangelization was the goal of the Society that saw its members as the equals of the holy women who served the apostles. These were the themes discussed among Mme Carré and the two residents of the House of the Good God. (Msgr. Laveille)

After a moment of doubt, the two associates regained confidence, and along with Fr. Chaumont, they saw in Mme Carré's leaving a perfect example of the renunciation he always tried to promote:

We have no shortage of trials to face: our Spiritual Mother, beloved of all her daughters, is leaving us for Rouen. But I think it is the will of our Lord that she remains as your mother. Even from a distance she will be able to watch over and encourage her little flock. I rejoice that God's work can be done in circumstances so unfavorable from a human point of view.[126]

I am going to tell you confidentially that your Spiritual Mother has been completely admirable in this situation. Once more she has given us the model of the strong woman. It would be impossible to put her poor nature more severely to the test. But she has responded with calm and joy, as the great Christian that she is. It is a dreadful blow for her heart. But it is an act of virtue that will bring great blessings from our Lord to our Association.[127]

Mme Carré was forced to reconcile her duties as a mother and her responsibilities in the Association. From her home in Rouen she took advantage of a trip to Arcueil, south of Paris where her son was in school, to visit the House of the Good God. Her husband declared his displeasure, saying that she was

---

[126]Letter from Henri Chaumont, May 29, 1874, in *Spiritual Letters*.
[127]Letter from Chaumont, June 23, 1874, in *Spiritual Letters*.

neglecting her family and her household. Fr. Chaumont wrote to him:

Sir: I am personally responsible in this situation. You are aware that Mme Carré has confided in me for the direction of her soul. No man preaches more fervently than I the exact fulfillment, conscientious, delicate, & supernatural, of the duties of marriage. To think for an instant that Mme Carré neglects these duties, that is, that she does not heed my counsel (but she is too sincere in her faith for that to be possible), or that I hold her to a different standard from the one that I preach to others, would offend me as a priest as much as you, as a soldier, would be offended if I suspected you of affirming outwardly a respect for the military that you undermined in practice. . . .

I congratulate you, sir, to have a wife who does not waste her time adorning herself, nor in futile conversations, nor in mindless reading as do so many other women. She devotes the little leisure time that she has to the direction of a project that will add to your name a nobility that comes straight from God. My duty has been fulfilled. As a priest I protest against any practices of the faith that would lead to neglecting the obligations of one's vocation. Because I am Mme Carré's spiritual director, I protest against certain insinuations that are being spread concerning the way she uses her time. And because you now know, sir, to what a beautiful work for God your wife devotes her little time spent here in Paris, I exhort you to bless the Lord for the good that is being done and to encourage her, not hiding from anyone how wonderfully useful you find the brief leisures that Mme Carré accords herself.[128]

In his biography of Mme Carré, Msgr. Laveille noted especially that the colonel's character vis-à-vis his wife became more bitter; he held her responsible for their son's initial failure to pass his baccalaureate examination, which kept him from entering the elite military school Saint-Cyr and for some problems that he experienced himself in the military world.

At the end of 1879, Colonel Carré decided to use a title of nobility that his family had taken in the past, "de Malberg," and having reached the age limit for his rank, decided to return definitively to Paris with his wife. He chose an apartment near the House of the Good God. He became more understanding and appreciative of his wife and more interested in matters of faith. Everything appeared to improve. Then, after a serious illness, Mme Carré was diagnosed with cancer. The disease seemed to be still in the beginning stages; there was hope to control it or that it would develop slowly. Fr. Chaumont informed his Daughters:

Our sister received this news like a true Daughter of the Spirit of Jesus. Her serenity, her calm, her goodness, her generosity have not changed in the least. She trusts entirely in God. Yes, praise God who has given this example through the Mother to all of her faithful Daughters. If the sickness progresses as we fear, in spite of the help of the doctor, the family will

---

[128] Letter from Chaumont to Colonel Carré, November 1877, quoted by Msgr. Laveille.

nevertheless ask God, with the intervention of his Saints, to save this good Mother. She will ask with so much faith that it will be granted, if God wills it. And if Jesus wants to take her, her Daughters will follow the example of her joyful resignation and with all of their hearts, say, "May God be praised." [129]

The Status of the Association

Fr. Henri Chaumont insisted on discretion in everything concerning the Daughters of St. Francis de Sales, and with good reason. These women constituted a group atypical for its time. They committed themselves as laypersons, whether single or married, to a way of life guided by the Gospels, leading to "the perfect life." Thus they promised, together and in the presence of a priest, their adherence to a group and to a particular way of living. Conscious of the uniqueness of such a commitment, the women maintained this discretion:

"We did not say that we belonged to a religious organization. I, for example, was teaching in public schools. It would not have been prudent in this milieu for it to be known that I had such a commitment." [130]

---

[129] H. Chaumont, *La Première Mère (The First Mother)*. Madame Carré also suffered the loss of her son Paul, who died from a horseback-riding accident, June 5, 1885; at the end of this same year, she lost her mother, whom she had cared for in her last months. After the initial pain of mourning, she regained her serenity little by little. "She learned to think of her son living close to God, having long and peaceful conversations with him that consoled her." (Laveille)

[130] Mlle Peccatte, in the *Summarium*.

Félicie Gros, also an elementary school teacher, reported a similar incident marking the lay state that the founder wanted to conserve for his Daughters:

In 1881 when religious education was eliminated from primary schools in Paris, [Fr. Chaumont] called us together (then there were three associates teaching in public schools); he asked us to remain there, emphasizing the example that we could give and asking that we each carry a crucifix in our pocket so that Jesus would always be present in the classroom.[131]

As a precaution, Fr. Chaumont consulted Fr. d'Hulst who had been made vicar general of Paris. The two men were conscious of the importance of evangelization by laywomen.[132] He agreed, in 1873, to be present at a meeting of the Daughters of St. Francis de Sales and promised to explain their organization to Cardinal Guibert, in order to allow it to live and thrive. Nevertheless, the cardinal remained hesitant, even if it is possible to imagine that the support of Fr. d'Hulst was decisive in gaining the difficult permission for the Daughters to continue. The vicar general told his friend, "You must have weighed the gravity of the situation you have put yourself in? You must succeed, you must succeed! Otherwise, the kindest thing we can

---

[131] *Summarium.*
[132] Although he was vicar general of Paris, he remained director of the organization of women catechists of Paris.

do for you is to put you away in some quiet and isolated corner of our dear diocese of Paris." [133]

However, when Msgr. Richard became archbishop coadjutor in 1875, he went in person to visit the House of the Good God and spoke encouragingly of the project. A relationship of confidence began between him and the Daughters. All the same, it was not until 1888, two years after Msgr. Richard had replaced Cardinal Guibert, that the new archbishop gave his approval. He had first taken the time to read the Rule of the Daughters, revised and completed, and the letters of approval from a great number of bishops. The canonical establishment was given on April 28, 1891.[134] Fr. d'Hulst and Fr. Chaumont continued to be cautious when they approached the subject of assigning an ecclesiastical mission to the Daughters.

It was premature to openly declare the existence of a group whose intention was to practice the virtues of a religious order while living in the world. It was impossible, without exposing ourselves to dangerous commentaries that might even kill the group in its cradle, to announce the creation of auxiliaries to parish priests.[135] The priests had not expressed the

---

[133] H. Chaumont, *La Première Mère*. Chaumont expressed his thanks to V.G. d'Hulst for the support he gave him at this juncture. He intimated that his friend had cautioned him to be very vigilant as to the quality of women he recruited in order to avoid any criticism that would be fatal to his undertaking.

[134] In this document the group is named as "an organization of pious persons."

[135] It was here that the plan for a collaboration between the Daughters and the Society of Priests of St. Francis de Sales saw the light. The idea was first expressed in 1874 (see Chapter VII).

desire for such auxiliaries and they in turn had not proven themselves. In the face of these difficulties, Fr. Chaumont decided to place the collective activities of the Daughters under the cover of a charitable organization with no suggestion of a relationship with a congregation of religious. Thus it could function openly. He had noted with sadness the frivolous way many of the women of the Faubourg Saint-Germain lived, claiming to act as Christians and at the same time indulging in practices far from a Christian way of life. . . . Hoping to put an end to such excesses, the priest decided to invite the women from the parish of Sainte Clotilde and the surrounding area to attend lectures and study, under his direction, how to live a Christian life as wives and mothers.

He imagined a "Society of Christian Women" that could have an official and open existence, recognized and even encouraged by the archbishop, but whose direction would be, discreetly, in the hands of his Daughters. It would help to bring a more solid Christian education to the women of this part of Paris and at the same time give some of his associates the possibility of collective evangelization under his direction. He spoke of the project to his friend Fr. d'Hulst who knew his secret and who defended him to the archbishop. He approved of the idea of a forceful reminder to the women of the upper classes of their responsibilities as Catholics and use of the cover it offered for the young society that needed to remain silent. (Msgr. Laveille)

The strategy is evident. To found a society of practicing Catholic women among the upper classes in

Paris seemed perfectly praiseworthy. The Daughters of St. Francis de Sales would support them as spiritual guides: This would be their first evangelizing mission, but they would not act as a formal group. Once they had established themselves by this action, they would be able to appear for what they really were. It is clear that Fr. Chaumont's intention was not only to encourage his Daughters to progress in their personal search for salvation, the primary goal of spiritual direction in the nineteenth century, but also to prepare them for evangelization. Alerting them to the difficulties that lay in wait for such a mission, he invited them to give themselves entirely to the salvation of others, in the footsteps of Christ, who had given his life on the cross, even though he suffered the incomprehension and ingratitude of those he loved:

Between souls and those who save them there is a communion of suffering and joy such that one cannot undertake effectively to save them without binding oneself to their fate. It is not only renunciation of self that is needed; it is devotion. In the name of our Lord, let those who are not ready to accept this mission withdraw now. Their place is not in our little Society. Let those who are afraid of crosses, leave now. This work will call for many crosses. We already have many; there will be more, more than in other undertakings. Let those who hope, through human prudence, to avoid crosses open their eyes. God loves our little association too much to let it perish. And it will perish the day it no longer needs to bear many crosses.

The souls to which you devote yourselves will especially try your faith. You will wonder time and time again where this sudden sadness comes from, these unwelcome temptations, these troubles, this distaste for the best things life offers, and especially, the goals of the Association. I can give you the answer in advance: You buy now the soul you will possess tomorrow. At other times, you will have worked hard to awaken a poor somnolent soul, to snatch a careless soul from danger, to sustain with patience a weak soul, and then, when you think the victory is won, it will all fall apart, or you will face a dreadful ingratitude. The explanation, I can tell you in advance: It is by the pain these cruel souls cause you that you will save them. [136]

The resolute tone of this text is striking. Fr. Chaumont is surely speaking from his own experience as a spiritual guide, telling his Daughters in all honesty what they must expect. Those who are looking only for peace and comfort in the Association are practically invited to leave. But it is rather to encourage and strengthen them that he underlines the difficulties they should expect as they begin their work of evangelization. At the same time, he is reminding them that the Association contributes to their own spiritual progress.

Msgr. Laveille reported that there appeared to be some questions of overlapping authority in the direction of the Association between the Spiritual Mother, Mme Carré, and the founder, who was at the same time her confessor. These differences concerned especially the admission of new members and were a reflection of

---

[136] Chaumont, letter of July 23, 1874, quoted by Msgr. Laveille.

their different temperaments as judges of people. Fr. Chaumont was quick to make a decision, Mme Carré more circumspect.[137]

It will always be easier for me to say "yes" and bend my own will before what our dear Father finds necessary than to see him close up on himself and say nothing once he has heard me express my point of view. His reserve is visible in those situations and it kills me; in fact, it paralyzes me all together.

Should I, when I fear a disagreement between our honored Father and myself, begin by asking him humbly what he thinks and what he wants, because then I would put all my good will to the task of thinking and judging and desiring what he does?" [138]

The Society of Christian Ladies

As we have seen, Fr. Chaumont continued to be concerned about the compatibility between life in worldly society and the spiritual life. He founded the Society of Christian Women,[139] which he entrusted to

---

[137] One day when she had with great discretion suggested to the priest that his decisions were too rapid, he told her that he had tried to find the cure for this failing, first by making up some rules that neither she nor he would have the right to break. But then he added, "That solution didn't seem to correspond to God's wishes. I abandoned it. Then I thought, maybe I should act more slowly. But I still wasn't satisfied with the answer." He went on: "My third thought was that you should submit to my decisions and that, my child, is the conclusion I arrived at." Letter dated July 4, 1883, cited by Msgr. Laveille.

[138] Unpublished letter, August 10, 1883, quoted by Msgr. Laveille.

[139] Its goals and rules are included in *Summarium*, pp. 549–555.

the guidance of the Daughters of St. Francis de Sales, meeting at the House of the Good God.

In the brochure presenting this project, he began by denouncing the incompatibility that some, even Christian families, perceived between the Gospel and worldly life. It was a perception that led them to see only two conclusions: worldly life as separate from the commands of God or the life of the cloister. Following the thought of St. Francis de Sales, he invited his contemporaries to move beyond this opposition. It is possible to live a fully Christian life in the world without fleeing our present times and escaping to the cloister.

The women who make up this Society, carefully chosen in light of its purposes, promise when they join:

To study seriously the duties they should fulfill in order to imitate the beautiful biblical image of the strong woman.[140]

To accept without resistance all of the laws of the Church and God, not only in theory but in their daily lives, remembering that faith, if it does not lead to observation of the commandments, is not enough to save our souls.

Take advantage of every situation to bring the Christian spirit to the secular world, especially in everything concerning maintaining a well-run household, raising children, and the art of receiving others with graciousness and generosity.

---

[140] This is a reference to Proverbs 31:10–31 and Sirach 26:1–18.

The women did not hide from the difficulties they would face in their humble undertaking. They did not expect to be pleasantly welcomed at all times; there might even be mean-spirited criticism, but they would consider themselves honored to be treated as our only Master and his saints were treated, and as all those who follow in his path are treated, happy that they are fleeing from the way of perdition in taking the path of the "narrow gate" that leads to Life.[141]

Fr. Chaumont, following the ideas of St. Francis de Sales, could not accept an easy compromise: He could not reconcile the Gospel with the spirit of the world, in the sense that St. John used the term. If the two are in conflict, the worldly life gives way before the commandments of the Gospel.

At first the Society of Christian Ladies had significant success. Fr. Chaumont gave three lectures each week, on a different subject: the Christian household, raising children, and the social graces. Mme Sallard reflected on the lectures.

Fr. Chaumont's words, trenchant, precise, sometimes fiery, captured and held the attention of the listeners, but his hope was to bring about concrete changes in the women's lives. However, these lessons, presented three times a week on both varied and delicate subjects, in which the priest was not a specialist, were draining his strength. It was a wonder that he was able to bear such a burden for a whole year. It also

---

[141] *The Society of Christian Women*, brochure.

included his inspirational talks to the Daughters and his service (as chaplain) to the Christian Brothers.

He had to give up some of these responsibilities. The next year he limited himself to one topic and spoke only once a week. The audience increased in number and the attraction of these talks, especially on the subject of "Maintaining a Christian Household" was so great that they were published in a volume.[142] (Msgr. Laveille)

The treatise, published in 1875, was titled *Managing a Christian Home*, followed by *Raising Children, Difficulties and Purposes* (1877).[143] Fr. Chaumont emphasized the role of the family in child-raising, suggesting that children remain at home while they study, in order to have the support of their mothers, rather than going to boarding schools. He especially denounced the use of too much art work or music and made lists of recommended books. In order to make his suggestions more attractive and accessible, he published a little monthly review originally titled *Christian Women* (1875) and later *The Christian Spirit* (1882).

---

[142] The goal was too ambitious. The priest was overwhelmed with work, and the lectures wore out the patience of his listeners. The next year he worked at a more modest pace. It is clear here that Fr. Chaumont was still leading the meetings with the Daughters, leaving them in a secondary role.

[143] Acknowledging the shortcomings of these works, especially their rather ponderous style, Msgr. Laveille calls them "treasures of acute observations, judicious advice, and even some perceptive insights into the future."

His intention was to give "timely counsels" based on Scripture, and inspired by a feast of the Church or the liturgical year or an annual event celebrated by social traditions. He also wrote texts intended for meditation, taken from his lectures, treating of the obligations of Christian women to family or society. He wrote of the obstacles posed by fashion or prejudice, and the abuses caused by incursions of the worldly spirit into a life of faith and good works.

These little missives encouraged examinations of conscience, and people came to the priest to discuss many issues that his articles caused them to consider, asking for his opinion. Judging that the responses to these consultations might have a general interest, Fr. Chaumont included a new rubric in his publication, "Questions and Answers," a list of solutions to the many questions of conscience arising in family life. These solutions, not found in books on theology, nor in works dealing with the daily practice of faith, drew the attention not only of the worldly society of Paris, but also of priests who were looking for answers to such difficulties. (Msgr. Laveille)

As the resolution of cases of conscience[144] was, in principle, the domain of recognized specialists in Christian morality, this initiative on the part of Fr. Chaumont irritated some sensibilities:

---

[144] To resolve a case of conscience is to give advice on making a moral decision about how to avoid the sin.

Fr. Chaumont's moral decisions were quoted even in meetings of Church authorities.[145] This exposed them to the criticism of a small number of ecclesiastics who were more inclined to severity than they were familiar with the exact rules of theology. His stances on some issues were judged too indulgent by some of the clergy so that a decision by judges who remained above the fray was necessary in order to reaffirm his approach to evangelization. (Msgr. Laveille)

However, it would be difficult to qualify the priest's tone as "indulgent" when he denounced in his review a certain number of practices of the well-off in worldly society:

1) *A month before the beginning of our next Lenten season, people in the most elegant salons will be saying that temperaments these days are anemic, so that dispensations for fasting and abstinence should be generously accorded. But at the same time, the weakest of our young ladies will be condemned to spend two or three nights a week in an atmosphere sickened by heat and the emanations of exotic plants, condemned to perform wild dances which doctors as well as theologians censor, further condemned to live*

---

[145] These conferences were the monthly meetings of priests from a given deanery, which included a study session where questions were set forth for discussion, on the basis of questionnaires sent out by the bishop. Corrected minutes of these meetings were sent to the bishop and sometimes put in printed form at the end of the year.
Sometimes "cases of conscience" were published anonymously in this document, since an important part of the ministry of these priests was the Sacrament of Penance.

irregular hours and lose the sleep that adolescents need so badly.

. . . . and the keepers of the traditions of worldly society will triumph from this state of affairs.

2) *Theaters will present the most risqué scenes, the most revolting exhibitions of morals, and in chorus, the public will say, "Great art is dead; how can they dare show us such things!" But, two months in advance, the boxes will be rented, and in the front row, you can see the elite of "good society," women who demand respect, and too often, their daughters sitting beside them, and their younger children will go to circuses in droves to see the most scandalous of things without blushing.*

Authors and theater directors will shrug their shoulders at the complaints of the moralizers, and continue to produce things even more absurd and revolting.[146]

However, over the years, Fr. Chaumont recognized the limits of these observations in the midst of the "Society of Christian Women." People listened to his lectures, but they did not so easily put into practice the words they professed to believe. His campaign against the dances[147] was a failure. Only one family agreed to

---

[146] Quoted by Msgr. Laveille.

[147] These were balls organized by the young people of several families in their various homes. These protests were not only the work of Fr. Chaumont. Msgr. Dupanlop (1802–1878), bishop of Orléans, senator, academician, and author of several well-

124

substitute other activities in the place of the dances so much in fashion. In the end, the "Society of Christian Ladies" ceased to exist between 1891 and 1895; only a sister society continued to exist until the First World War in 1914. It was difficult for Fr. Chaumont to accept the failure of this attempt at evangelization in a privileged milieu, whose spiritual needs seemed so clear to him. He tried again with the "Society of Christian Widows" with the support of the Daughters of St. Francis de Sales. They organized lectures and held meetings through the First World War. He also formed other groups of women of strong faith who could carry the Gospel message to different social classes.[148]

Probations

Probably during one of his spiritual retreats, Fr. Chaumont came across a little religious text, titled *Probations,* which was intended as a guide for novices entering religious communities. After consulting his Council, he decided to adopt this method of formation for the candidates wishing to enter the Society of Daughters and the Society of Priests.

The method is based on two principles: 1) the obligation to instruct the novices[149] thoroughly and

---

received works on education and parenting, also wrote against attending these dances in his city: *Lectures for Christian Women.*
[148] For each of these groups, which lasted for a greater or shorter period of time, he made up a Rule for: Christian teachers, nurses aides, young under civil protection, circus performers.
[149] These are the persons who have asked to enter one or another society. The term "novitiate" refers to the time before

guide them in the exercises of the life of perfection, with reference to their particular vocation; 2) the requirement not to burden the postulants with too many exercises, since they were living active lives in society. They had only short intervals in which to perform these disciplines.[150]

For these reasons, Fr. Chaumont returned to ideas already published as the *Spiritual Direction of Saint Francis de Sales,* now with the title *Probations.* He worked with several associates, two of whom were leaders of a recently founded group in Dijon. The project was hastily prepared and needed some revision, undertaken by Fr. Costaz, who took over the direction of the Daughters.[151] Thus the method was brought to the attention of superiors of many religious congregations who in turn asked Fr. Chaumont for copies of the publication. Fr. Landon adapted the exercises for use by the Priests of St. Francis de Sales. Humility and obedience were among the qualities that the founder hoped to develop in his associates. He often cited the model of the Jesuits, who accepted a change of responsibilities or a reassignment without question. Above all, he insisted on love: "I would pardon everything, of everyone, except one thing: forgetting love. Love is your distinctive note, your

---

their definitive acceptance. Today the term "aspirant" is more frequently used.

[150] *Notes and Souvenirs offered by the Council to Members of the Society.*

[151] First a priest in the diocese of Belley, he continued his ministry in Paris. It was he who began the cause for the canonization of Mme Carré.

special grace, the fundamental character of your vocation.[152]

The society took "Love is the fulfillment of the law" [153] as its motto.

Spirit and Organization of the Society

In 1889, with the Society of the Daughters of St. Francis de Sales springing up in the provinces, Fr. Chaumont needed to give more structure to the organization.

One of the members of the General Council had the title of "General Director of Novices." The priest had to instruct the directors in the provinces (Regionals) and ensure communication among them so that all Daughters would have the same formation. The founder insisted on a degree of centralization so that all, novices [Aspirants and Probanists] as well as those who made it their profession [consecration], would be penetrated with the same spirit.

The development of the society led Fr. Chaumont to accord to Mme Carré, as she asked, two "auxiliaries" who were named "general assistants." He had also to define more precisely the role of "spiritual mothers." They are now known as "Probatrices or Companions." Their responsibility is to assist the new members in the exterior practice of the Rule, to point out failings or eccentricities, but always to respect personal consciences.

---

[152] Talk given to the Council, June 3, 1885, cited by Msgr. Laveille.
[153] *The Exercise of Love,* meditation 27.

We clearly see here the distinction, inherited from the French school of spirituality, separating the external (*externe*) from the internal (*intérieur*). The former indicates conduct that is openly observable by all, that the *Probatrices* could regulate, while the latter refers to questions of conscience that should be shared only with the spiritual director. Due to the mobilization during the First World War, women took a more important place in French society and also in the Church, because so many priests were serving with the military. The Daughters of St. Francis de Sales were able to perform an important service to the clergy. Making the interior/exterior distinction clear, chaplain Henri Colin reassured his fellow priests that the *Probatrices* in no way usurp the role of spiritual directors; they make their work easier:

This needs to be made very clear: The usefulness and the exact role of the Probatrices are not always understood. Their institution sometimes causes anxieties, criticism, or even defiance. Without in any way interfering with the action of the spiritual director, a Daughter is a guide, a doctor of the soul, a spiritual friend, discreet and devoted, fulfilling an important if circumscribed function. Is the busy priest able to deal with all of the details, the secondary questions of entering into the Salesian formation? Is he always able to explain to those in his charge everything concerning the practices and documents of the Association? Should he not be happy to leave a soul who has been confided to him in the care of a Probatrice, one who is prudent, loving, even from time to time a consolation inspired by God?

. . . . To avoid as much as possible, the errors and abuses that can filter into the best of things, the Daughters called to be Probatrices were very carefully chosen, prepared with great prudence and attention. They were reminded never to venture into areas that were properly those of the director of conscience, never solicit confidences. If they heard them, they were instructed to respond with extreme discretion, so as to give the associates an example of deference and complete confidence in their directors.

Thus it is clear that the role of the Probatrice is a service to the priest: Many external things in the social sphere escape the spiritual director, even if the person is sincere and open with her confessor.

On the other hand, a woman notices rapidly, in conversation, in correspondence, faults or errors, habits that can be hurtful, but also conduct that should be encouraged and developed, helpful for herself and her family and friends. Little by little the Probatrice, whose mission is to ensure the observation of the Rule, will find a way to point out with kindness any weakness that she has noticed. This spiritual friendship has a good influence on souls having a sincere desire to become true Daughters of St. Francis de Sales.[154]

In a letter to Msgr. Lelong, bishop of Nevers, Fr. Chaumont himself had given the same analysis of the relationship of the Daughters to the clergy:

---

[154] H. Colin, "The Society of Daughters of Saint Francis de Sales," *Bulletin,* June 1917.

The Daughters of St. Francis de Sales have a double mission: to practice a Christian life wherever the Providence of God has placed them and lead souls toward the priest who in turn will lead them to Jesus, or help them to grow in the love of our Lord. . . . To reach the first goal, the women have the following means: the Holy Eucharist, received in daily attendance at Mass; visits to the Blessed Sacrament; firm but gentle spiritual guidance by priests "filled with love, wisdom and prudence"; [Introduction to the Devout Life]; constant reading of the Gospels, of the Catechism, and of St. Francis de Sales; and a special formation of at least two years, reinforced with meetings whenever possible, and in any case by the instructions given here and in seven successive probations. This program is conceived in such a way as never to interfere with a candidate's duties as a wife and mother. To become a Daughter of St. Francis de Sales is always an accomplishment that is conscientious, devout, and punctilious in the fulfillment of her duties.

The second goal is achieved by the following methods: A Daughter gives herself as much as possible to the service of souls. She always feels the obligation to give an example of a truly Christian life: She loves to instruct the ignorant, to visit the poor and the sick who may be brought to her attention.

When this is done, she defers to the ministry of the priest who must leave souls their necessary independence. The Daughter never mistakes her role for that of the director of conscience.

A Daughter's role is one of humility and love. But it is important to add that a priest finds here a very useful institution. On the one hand, good works are no longer confided to persons with no instruction, often lacking prudence or discretion, who can harm the cause of religion that they intend to serve. On the other hand, many details that the priest may overlook at his risk, are spared him. With all discretion, he can follow and support souls that may perish, that he could not go in search of, but who are led to him for the work of salvation.[155]

Fr. Chaumont thought that the Daughters' role should be essentially that of auxiliaries to priests; he believed that his authority and that of other priests who directed the groups took precedence over the opinions of the Councils of the members, even though the Councils were always consulted. In an exhortation on November 7, 1883, he put the Council on guard against an independence of action that could be harmful, but he called on the members not to abdicate their role. The Associates have the obligation to express their opinion in order to help those who have ultimate authority form a mature judgment.

We ask the Council to maintain the full independence of their vote and their opinions. It is important that we know your point of view. We often find important insights in these ideas. Your role is not to be overlooked. But we also ask that you remain

---

[155] Letter of Fr. Chaumont to Msgr. Lelong, September 18, 1882, quoted by Msgr. Leveille.

dependent and know how to sacrifice your judgment with humility and the spirit of faith.[156]

Expansion of the Society of the Daughters of Saint Francis de Sales

Several groups were formed quite rapidly outside of Paris and beyond. Starting in 1874, thanks to the summers that Mlle de Parieu spent in her native town, a group began at Aurillac, south of Paris, with the cooperation of Fr. Delort; it was formed around a group of young girls who used their leisure time repairing the church vestments.[157] Another group began at Bréménil in the Vosges, thanks to Mlle Poussardieu and to the priest, Fr. Mienville, who encouraged the habit of frequent Communion among his parishioners. Fr. Chaumont sketched the beginning and character of this group:

Beginning in 1873, a woman from very humble origins—she was a domestic servant—entered the Society of Daughters. She was deeply attached to the Association, meditated often on the question of how to establish the Society in the Vosges, in the little village where she was born. The parish of Bréménil was led by a deeply spiritual and intelligent priest, who had decided to dedicate his life to pursuits requiring endless work and no human ambition for the future. There are many such priests who find satisfaction of a

---

[156] Quoted by Msgr. Laveille.

[157] Henri Chaumont related the history of this foundation in his book *La Premiere Mere*, the spiritual biography of the founder. Célestine Gallut was revered as a saintly woman; he adds that some healings were attributed to her intercession.

132

much higher nature, in guiding docile and fervent souls.

[Mlle Poussardieu], who knew the great faith of this priest, asked permission to explain the work of the Daughters to him. She left for her village with this mission and found all the success she dared to hope for. Fr. Chaumont went first to Bréménil to speak with the parish priest, who returned the visit, going to Paris where he completed his instruction in Salesian spirituality. Soon this village of four hundred souls had a good number of Daughters of St. Francis de Sales. Their formation reflected the character of their home region; it had an exceptional energy and reverence for Fr. Chaumont. Under this surface, where some might well have looked for the spirit of the good and gentle St. Francis de Sales, the priest of Bréménil taught his Daughters the doctrine of the blessed bishop of Geneva, according them willingly frequent Communion and making them living examples of Christian virtue and apostleship. [158]

Mlle de Malaret in the parish of Saint Sernin in Toulouse and Mlle Solignac in Dijon also began groups of associates.

There was also a small number of women of British origin. One of them, Miss Toneri, appeared one day at the Council carrying in her arms the statue of the Infant Jesus that had lain in the oratory of the House of the Good God from Christmas to the feast of St. Francis de Sales. She was asking permission to carry it to London, where she could ensure it a permanent

---

[158] Henri Chaumont, *La Premiere Mere.*

133

veneration. She reassured the Council that Providence would reward this act of confidence by bringing the Society to England. Her request showed such fervent faith that the Council granted her this way to search out God's designs. Three months later the Catholic priest of Southampton asked for some Daughters who could assist him in his ministry. Soon a second group was founded in the outskirts of the city, at Woolston, preparing the ground for another group that took root in London proper, in the poor sector of Wapping. And before that group had time to be completely established, the Daughters were present at Autun, Nancy, Meaux, Fontainebleau, Bourg, Mortagne, au Havre, and Dieppe. Making voyage after voyage, Fr. Chaumont could hardly give enough time for a blessing and a welcome to the new groups that asked for his presence. (Msgr. Laveille)

During the process of beatification, Miss Toneri told of her memories of the beginnings of the mission in England—her meeting with an English governess in Paris who wanted to abjure her faith, to whom Fr. Chaumont sent her. In 1879, she set up her first residence in Southampton. Once they were there, they met a Catholic priest who at first would not accept their apostolate. But the priest, serving the military hospital in the nearby town, called them three months later. He offered them a house with a garden and another building that they could use as a school during the week and a chapel on Sundays. In London, at Wapping, they were better received, but the situations they encountered there were difficult:

In 1884, a priest who had heard of the good we were doing in Woolston wrote directly to Fr. Chaumont asking that he send a group. I translated the letter and volunteered to go. Our arrival in Wapping was very different from what happened at Southampton. The priest asked us right away to visit the parish, where there were about two thousand Catholics. We were warmly welcomed everywhere. The mission in Wapping lasted nine years; the harvest was abundant. There were conversions and marriages saved; we could no longer count the number of Baptisms. The priest was obliged to ask for two assistants. We faced much suffering and privation because we were living at the very center of the worst strike that had taken place in London in 1888. Families were nearly dying of hunger. Every day we saw processions of between sixty and eighty thousand starving men. It was to the glory of the great and saintly Cardinal Manning that he was able to end the strike. In 1894 our Sisters were called back to Paris, where I had returned three years earlier. We were replaced by the Sisters of St. Vincent de Paul, who are continuing what we began. (Summarium)

On the occasion of a retreat preached to the priests of his diocese in Nevers, Fr. Tissot informed Msgr. Lelong of the existence of the Societies of Priests and Daughters. The bishop called them immediately. In response, Fr. Chaumont sent his sister, Marthe, who was able to start a group very quickly. It was recognized by the bishop, who confided it to the chancellor of the diocese in 1884. The Daughters rented a house and installed a chapel, thinking that they would be able to form Catechist Missionaries. As it turned out, there was no priest available at Nevers to take charge of their instruction; the candidates had to be sent to Paris, so the house was closed. Understandably the Daughters were discouraged.

As for Lyon, once they had overcome the objections of Cardinal Cavérot,[159] Fr. Chaumont and the Council decided to send one of the most reliable Daughters, Mlle Stiltz, to direct the group that had begun with the inspiration of two priests from the Salesian family, Frs. Bonnardet and Nugue. In spite of her health, Mlle Stiltz accepted the mission. In fact, her condition worsened several times, to the point where her doctors wanted to send her to Hyères.[160] But she remained in Lyon to help the "spiritual mothers" in the preparation of forty-six new members. (October 1884)

In 1889, there were 736 Daughters of St. Francis de Sales; in 1895 there were 1,761; and in 1900, there were more than 2,000. Logically, Mlle Stiltz took over as general directress of the Society, elected to the office in 1891. She worked both to make the work of the first "Spiritual Mother" better known and to obtain papal approval of the Society. In spite of her frail health, she lived to be seventy-five.

On April 26, 1911, Pope Pius X published a decree approving the Rule of the Society. In the letter that he addressed to Mlle Stiltz, he recognized explicitly the

---

[159] He was afraid that the priests of St. Francis de Sales would only obey their superior in Paris and that the Daughters would claim that they themselves were spiritual directors.
[160] Two years after her arrival, she was struck by a paralysis of her lower limbs.

lay character of the Daughters and its double purpose: sanctification and evangelizing, in the role of auxiliaries of the priesthood.[161] He approved as well the pedagogy of the *probations:*

The membership of this Association includes not only young women and widows but also married women, which differentiates it absolutely from religious congregations. It has two goals: the sanctification of each of its members and a constant apostolate, both of which correspond to the wishes of our heart.

In order to fulfill these goals entirely, it uses methods that are as efficient as they are legitimate. First of all, the sanctification of each woman is faithfully guided by the probations. . . .

As for evangelization, it concerns principally the good example to be given to our fellows, be they in the family, among those near to us, in works of charity and even in the farthest reaches of the earth. These works, too numerous to list here, of all kinds, are always appropriate for the people and the places to be served. This mission makes all Daughters worthy and devoted auxiliaries of the clergy, in teaching catechism, in the protection of faith and morals, in easing temporal suffering, and in the development of Christian life. For

---

[161] Although the Daughters are here called "auxiliaries," a word that underlines their inferior status in the hierarchy, an evolution took place leading to a new vocabulary, "collaboration with the apostolic hierarchy," applied by Vatican Council II. (Decree *Apostolican actuositatem, no. 20* concerning the apostolate of such groups as Catholic Action.)

these reasons the Society from the beginning has grown most beautifully." [162]

Death of Madame Carré de Malberg

Even though he remained the spiritual director of Mme Carré, to whom he preached "humility, detachment, and generous love," Fr. Chaumont demonstrated great confidence in her judgment, even in questions concerning the Priests of St. Francis de Sales.

It is curious to see, in his correspondence with Mme Carré, how deeply they were both committed to this project and how much the spiritual Father counted on the prayers of the woman whose spiritual director he was in order to find the graces he needed for the Society of Priests. He kept Mme Carré informed of all his preliminary steps, of the first men who came forward with interest in the association, and who were welcomed with great joy. He humbled himself with her; that is, he revealed himself to her, as he saw himself, as all should see themselves, in the presence of God, with whatever authority our Lord chooses to bestow on us. The priest saw himself as weak, his own misery; he thought that the meager success of his undertakings was the result of his own imperfections and that he could do little in proportion to the divine grace he received.

But these revelations on the part of a priest made to a woman of great faith were made under conditions so unique and in such a particular way that their roles

---

[162] Letter from Pope Pius X to Marie Stiltz, quoted by Msgr. Laveille in *Mme Carré de Malberg*.

were in no way reversed. If the spiritual director asked this remarkable soul to speak to our Lord about the Society of Priests of the Spirit of Jesus, it was because he knew that this project was dear to our Divine Master. Moreover, he knew that this soul under his direction received such favors from our Lord that he could without impropriety ask her to communicate God's will to him. He even asked Mme Carré to pray to God "to ask if we should think of some of the priests living in community." (Msgr. Debout)

Mme Carré's cancer took a turn for the worse in March 1890. The doctors despaired of the possibility of healing her, and in June suggested that she return to her family property in Lorry, near Metz, in eastern France. During this time, Fr. Chaumont who had been away preaching a retreat for the Priests of St. Francis de Sales, was extremely worried by the health of his sister Marthe. He went first to Paris before leaving for Lorry on September 28.

He found Mme Carré exhausted and in such unbearable pain that with the priest at Lorry he thought it was time to administer the last rites.

After hearing her say that she didn't want healing any more than she desired death, he asked again:

"Isn't there something that you want?"

Mme Carré closed her eyes and reflected.

"Father, I have asked myself conscientiously and I have to say that I can find nothing to desire."

She repeated that she wished neither for life nor for health.

Her director insisted, "At least that your pain be relieved?"

"Neither that nor anything else, Father. I only feel what I have always felt through so many years of service to God; but I feel that deeply. I love only His adorable will. That is all I can wish; I don't even feel the desire to will something else." (Msgr. Laveille)

Since he had to return to Paris, Fr. Chaumont asked Mlle Stiltz to come to Lorry to be with Mme Carré. The younger woman was struck by the changes in the First Spiritual Mother. Shortness of breath and attacks of rheumatism kept Fr. Chaumont from leaving the capital. He asked Mlle Stiltz and another assistant, Mlle Anquier, to return to Lorry, with this message for Mme Carré:

"Go to God, my child. Go humbly, gently, like a true daughter, in confidence and joy. Go to meet so many other dear ones who have gone before; go and wait for these worldly and spiritual families who will follow you until one day all together at that holy meeting place, we will sing, 'Live Jesus.'" [163]

The two women who were caring for Mme Carré saw her join her hands, calling out,

"My Jesus, I die giving all my heart and all my soul. I have given up everything because I have given you

---

[163] Letter of Fr. Chaumont to Mme Carré, January 24, 1891, quoted by Msgr. Laveille.

everything. I die in reparation for all the times I have not accepted your will, for everything that I have not done perfectly." [164]

After the death of Mme Carré, January 28, 1891, Fr. Chaumont decided to tell his other Daughters the full beauty of their founding mother, by composing in one year and in the intervals left by his many occupations, her spiritual biography. Reading the book, Fr. Debout commented, *"I had the happiness to meet this woman and to visit her for several years. The gentle impression that her conversation left with me told me even then that she was a saint. But I didn't know that she had reached such a point of perfection."* [165]

Struck by the witness to supernatural favors that had served Fr. Chaumont in writing his book, Mlle Stiltz expressed the idea of beginning a procedure toward beatification. At her request and that of Chaplain Costaz, a member of the Society of Priests and a canonist and compiler of the dossier for the Curé of Ars, a commission of members of the Society of Priests was assembled, with the charge to gather testimonies. The dossier was given to Msgr. Fleck, bishop of Metz, so that the ordinary first step toward beatification could begin on January 7, 1896. Several examples of healings attributed to the First Spiritual Mother were presented. For three years the commission working in the diocese of Metz heard more than forty witnesses. The documents were sent to Rome in August 1898 to be examined by the Congregation of Rites. On June 23, 1909, Pope Leo

---

[164] Quoted by Msgr Laveille.
[165] Quoted by Msgr. Laveille.

XIII signed the decree of introduction of the cause, allowing that Mme Carré receive the title of "venerable" [according to the rules of the times]. The apostolic process began in Metz and in Paris in 1911, and the decree of *fama sanctitatis* (the reputation of saintliness) was handed down November 16, 1915, and the validation on December 18, 1929. The *positio* declaring the heroic nature of her virtues was presented March 13, 1997. On May 9, 2014, Pope Francis authorized the promulgation on the "Decree of Heroic Virtues of Caroline Barbe Colchen Carré de Malberg. Under the modified rules now in effect, the decree is necessary to confer the title of venerable.

The Society of Christian Teachers

We have seen how both Fr. Mermillod and Fr. Brisson were concerned about education. The same was true for the Daughters of St. Francis de Sales and especially Mme Carré. She suggested founding a normal school for Catholic elementary school teachers. The project began with a new series of lectures by Fr. Chaumont to the Daughters concerning, first of all, the qualities necessary to fulfill this vocation, and then on the ways to have a beneficial influence on the minds of children.[166] The priest ended with some discussion of the relationship between the teacher and parents of pupils. Chaumont published a book based on these talks, *Instructions for Christian Primary School*

---

[166] "A study of the primary weakness, the action of prayer, vigilance and punishments, formation of sensitivity and character: all of these points were the subject of observations, analysis, and advice taken from the experiences of the best-known educators of his time." Msgr. Laveille

Teachers (2nd edition, 1886). Starting with one of the Daughters, Mlle Gros, a *Society of Christian Teachers* began; with the help of Fr. Chaumont it developed to a certain degree and lasted through World War I.

The Association of the Servants to Priests

This organization, also an outgrowth of the Daughters of St. Francis de Sales, lasted only a short time. It was initiated by Fr. Chaumont and Mlle Parieu, with the purpose of forming housekeepers for priests, who would be devoted to their work and satisfied to earn a modest salary.

A Rule was drawn up, and the task was offered to a few young women very faithful to the Church, who would feel honored to serve their priests. A small group did in fact materialize, but the Society of Daughters was not strong enough to encourage this project. Very quickly problems began to surface in the residences; it was difficult to recruit the necessary personnel. The project had to be abandoned even though it seemed to be so promising for the Church, the priesthood, and those who served the priests. (Msgr. Laveille)

After the First World War, this project was tried again, as well as another short-lived group founded by Fr. Chaumont, Christian Caregivers to the Sick.

Evangelization of Non-Christian Women

Starting in his childhood, Henri Chaumont was an assiduous reader of the *Annals of the Propagation of the Faith;* as a seminarian he was struck by the fate of women in countries that were in the process of evangelization—that they were kept from contact with a priest by local customs. He read the appeals of apostolic vicars asking for help for Christian women at least in the form of prayer. This was his starting point:

From his seminary days . . . , he had been concerned by the situation of non-Christian women. The preoccupation remained with him. One day he called Mme Sallard, who was already partly responsible for the Society of Christian Women. He spoke to her in emotional terms of the unhappiness of these women living without knowledge of God, asking her if she would like to devote herself to helping them through constant prayer but also by offering up all of the pain she suffered because of a grumpy and taciturn husband. (Msgr. Laveille)

He also met Mlle Cardou, who shared his concern. Together they organized a campaign of prayer for the salvation of these non-Christian women. He awakened the interest of some Carmelites and other congregations. During their vacation in 1880, Mlle Cardou and Mlle Gros, founder of a Salesian group at Fontainebleau, traveled though Brittany in far western France, to gather people to work in the cause. They achieved 1,800,000 promises of prayer. Fr. Chaumont placed this project under the patronage of Immaculate Mary, and a notice was widely distributed explaining the goals of this campaign.[167] On December 8, 1893,

---

[167] *Mission for the Salvation of Uninstructed Women through the Merciful Heart of Jesus and Mary Immaculate.* Before 1889, Fr. Chaumont founded a review to encourage the work of prayer

the society had more than 200,000 members, many of whom worked as catechists in their parishes. Their number continued to increase in the following decades.[168]

In 1903 Fr. Feige, a priest in the diocese of Meaux, and director of the Society of Immaculate Mary, founded an Association of Mary Immaculate whose goal was to prepare young women for marriage according to the methods of St. Francis de Sales, bringing to fruition a wish of Mme Carré, which the Spiritual Father had entrusted to her.[169]

The Catechist Missionaries in Non-Christian Countries

Prayer led naturally to action. Fr. Chaumont and Mme Carré heard the call for collaboration from the bishop of Canton, Msgr. Chausse, and one of his missionaries, Fr. Berthon, who had come into contact with the House of the Good God during a visit to Paris. The Daughters studied the question, but in the face of all the practical problems that the missionary noted, it seemed prudent to wait. Nevertheless, another call came in September 1889, from Msgr. Riccaz, bishop of Nagpur, India. He was a member of the Society of Missionaries of St. Francis de Sales, directed by Fr. Tissot. The four associates, who had been preparing

and to recruit Catechist Missionaries: *The Annals of the Society of Mary Immaculate.*
[168] In 1917, Msgr. Laveille spoke of more than 300,000 members.
[169] In 1917, groups with this purpose existed; Association of Mary Immaculate existed in Paris, Lyon, Nice, Grenoble, Chambéry, Montpellier, Périgeux Dôle, and Saint-Étienne-de-Tinée. (Alpes-Maritimes)

for several months to leave for China, agreed to change their plans and go to India. Writing from Lourdes, this message came from Fr. Chaumont:

Go, then, my Daughters, spread afar, even to the ends of the earth, the modest but saving practices of St. Francis de Sales. As the first Christian women, our elder sisters in the faith, went to Gaul, where your mothers were slaves and scorned; go in your turn, to teach these unfortunate women, bringing them the salvation of the humble and gentle Lord Jesus. Without you they would be unaware, throughout their lives, of what you have learned about the infinite mercies of the Heart of Jesus. Go tell them that, like you, they have the right to human dignity, the respect of all, the practice of the highest virtue, of the most beautiful devotion. Go tell them, "You were not even thinking of salvation, We will make you the apostles of salvation. You had no grace; now you will go to enrich others with your overabundance of grace. Go to harvest the blessings that your sisters here can never know." [170]

These few words reflect the attitude of the time that Christianity is a religion of salvation acting in the world as a civilizing process, especially working to free women from a condition of slavery in non-Christian societies.

Fr. Chaumont's touching appeal caused the House of the Good God to be caught up in the emotion of the approaching departure. All of the Associates and even their friends from the outside knew the travelers: Mlle

---

[170] Letter of Fr. Chaumont, in Lourdes, on eve of the Month of the Rosary, September 30, 1889, quoted by Msgr. Laveille.

Félicie Gros was already loved and venerated under the name of Mother Marie Gertrude; Sister Marie de Kostka was a former superior of the House of the Good God;[171] Sister Madeleine of the Holy Sacrament was leaving many dear ones in order to accompany the missionaries; and Sister Joseph of the Visitation, was one of the first women to join the group in Lyon.

Msgr. Richard himself had given the missionaries a sanctified stone, so that Mass could be celebrated as soon as possible in their future residence. Mother Marie Gertrude wanted to go with her companions to thank him and say good bye. . . . Extending his hand over the four women kneeling before him, he said, simply but with a voice full of tenderness, "Go, my dear Daughters. I give you the mission," and he blessed them.[172]

After a farewell Mass at the House of the Good God and a pause at Notre Dame de Fourvière in Lyon, the first four missionaries arrived in Marseilles, where they met Fr. Chaumont, who had come from Toulouse. On October 12, the Spiritual Father celebrated Mass with them at Notre Dame de la Garde; at the end of the day they boarded the ship the *Amazone*. Indeed, they were on their way. Once in Nagpur they saw the reality of this new country, the caste system and the ever-

---

[171] Miss Pilinska, of Polish origin.

[172] There again we must be attentive to the vocabulary. In spite of the terms used, the Catechist Missionaries were not a religious congregation. They became a congregation in 1968 under the name of Salesian Missionaries of Mary Immaculate.

present misery. At first they could only open a dispensary in a half-ruined building.

Very soon, vagabonds eaten by leprosy, children infected with ring worm, and cart-drivers half-blind from the burning dust of the roads came in droves to this refuge where the European sisters found a way to ease their suffering and sometimes to cure their ills. But the souls remained closed. On rare occasions an outcast woman would abandon her sick child to the nurses without a specific prohibition to Baptizing it. But even in these conditions, it was not until 1890 they were able to perform their first Baptism. (Msgr. Laveille)

Monseigneur (Bishop) Riccaz hoped to limit the Daughters to the role of nurses, but Fr. Chaumont had intended that they begin an apostolate. The latter called on the intercession of Fr. Tissot, superior of the family of religious to which the bishop belonged, and thus the difficulty was resolved. The bishop granted greater freedom of action to the women and they took some initiatives:

Without abandoning their dispensary, they began to make visits of evangelization around the city. They could be seen, sometimes on foot, sometimes crowded into an oxcart, making their way through the groups of hovels scattered among the rice paddies. Young Indians served as their interpreters, and their little bags of candy attracted the children. The people were at first terrorized at their approach, but soon they came near to take advantage of their medicine. After two months they had been able to perform two Baptisms. . . . The bishop asked that they open an asylum for widows and schools and centers for small children. Through their work with widows, they were at last reaching the women whose lives they most wanted to touch. The schools would bring them the future generations. (Msgr. Laveille)

A second group left for Canton, in the south of China on October 5, 1890, led by Mother Angéline of the Sacred Heart. Msgr. Chaussse asked them to administer an orphanage, with the help of some indigenous Christian women known as "Christian Virgins." The Daughters used the practices of their Society in order to instruct these women, and the results were very good. Soon their house was home to forty-five young Chinese women whom they hoped to prepare as catechists, and every month about one hundred children were brought to them for Baptism. Fr. Chaumont saw the difficulties that these first missionary Daughters faced and realized that they had to have superior spiritual strength. He also saw the need for more practical preparation, especially to teach literacy.

The group in Canton could not survive, but the one in Nagpur grew and was able to spread to the peninsula of Hindustan. Looking back over the accomplishments of this Society of Mary Immaculate, for the year 1893, Msgr. Laveille notes some success: hundreds of Baptisms in Nagpur and Canton, the opening of two centers to teach aspirant-missionaries in Lyon and Brussels, and the results of the work in Paris of the Catechist Missionaries. They dealt there with abjurations, performed Baptisms, and prepared First Communions. In November 1894, they opened a new center in Madagascar, in very difficult material conditions.

The following year, Fr. Chaumont recalled Mlle Gross (Mother Marie Gertrude) from her position as Superior in Nagpur so that she could work with the Association of Mary Immaculate. She returned with a young Indian woman, and the Society began a new development that led to a new foundation in Dacca (now the capital of Bangladesh) and extension of the foundation in Madagascar. In 1900 the missionaries opened a center in Kimbakonum, India, and then in 1914, in Bangalore, where they created schools, orphanages, and workshops.

Fr. Chaumont preached a retreat to the Catechist Missionaries who were about to leave, a "Retreat of Death." Mary-Louise Langlois described it in this way:

It was like the death of the will that St. Francis de Sales speaks of. He divided the retreat into three days:

1)   death to material things
2)   death to human affections
3)   death to the self

At the end he gave this last warning, "If you still are holding onto something, it would be better for you to put off your departure. You should be in such a state of mind and heart that even if you were already on your way and you were ordered to return to Paris, you would be ready to do so immediately and give up your desire to be missionaries." (Summarium)

The Catechist Missionaries in Christian Lands

Fr. Chaumont called for prayers not only for women who had no contact with Christianity but also for those in Christian countries who lived in heresy, in schism, or far removed from religion. Conscious of the needs for missionary work in France, he proposed a new field of endeavor to the Council of his Daughters on July 10, 1891.

Isn't it possible that God's will could be not only to send our sisters to faraway lands but also that we prepare them to serve the multitude of souls living without Baptism in Paris and in our other big cities? The Little Sisters of the Assumption perform many Baptisms, and regularize marriages, but they cannot do all that is needed. If we could also reach out in the name of "The Holy Childhood,"[173] for the interests of the little children without religion in the heart of Paris, a great good would be accomplished.[174]

The Catechist Missionaries were sent to parishes in Paris and the suburbs, where they organized feasts of patron saints, catechisms, and visits to families, especially in the Lenten season, or during parish missions.[175] The women collaborated easily with the Daughters of St. Francis de Sales. On January 30,

---

[173] An organization founded in 1843 by Msgr. de Forbin-Janson, to encourage the Baptism of infants in mission countries and to buy back and educate slave children.

[174] Manuscript minutes of the meeting of the Council, July 10, 1891, quoted by Msgr. Laveille.

[175] These events were intended to persuade families to go to church and listen to the sermons given for that liturgical occasion.

1893, Fr. Chaumont awarded the cross to the first three "missionaries to Christian lands." Marie Agnès Hébrand de Villeneuve told what happened afterward:

Ten days before his death, at the Council of May 5, 1896, Fr. Chaumont approved the foundation of our first Mission House in Paris at 17 rue Linné, near the Jardin des Plantes and the University of Jussieu. It did not open until October, at the same time as the houses at Alfrort and Plaisance. The dispersion of rue de Bourgogne, the persecutions of religious congregations at that time obliged the groups to be very prudent. They remained in the shadows for some time, but now there are several houses carrying out the mission. (Summarium)

Another Daughter, Mary-Gertrude Lévy, a convert to Catholicism from Judaism, wanting to live a life of devotion but neither in marriage nor as a religious sister, was sent by Fr. Chaumont with several other women to the house in Notre Dame du Rosaire.[176] (Summarium)

Fr. Chaumont had certainly not forgotten his experience with the working class of Paris at Saint Marcel. Thus he saw with great concern the abandonment of the Church taking place among this group, even though the people still brought their children to be baptized. The Catechist Missionaries thus turned especially to encouraging feasts of patron

---

[176] The pastor, Fr. Soulange-Bodin, was a member of the Society of Priests of St. Francis de Sales.

saints and parish missions.[177] The Catechist Missionaries brought their support to the feasts and collaborated with the parish missions. These were principally the responsibility of parish priests, who were organized by the Society of Missionary Dioceses of Paris, a group begun by Fr. Lenfant but directed by Fr. Gibergues, the personal secretary of Cardinal Richard.[178]

The Sons of Saint Francis de Sales

The creation of this group seemed the next logical step after the creation of the Daughters. It took place in 1887, even though Fr. Chaumont had first had the idea ten years earlier.[179] He confided the direction of the group to Fr. Emmanuel de la Perche (1845–1932).

The Sons were always to look for inspiration in the spirit of the Gospels, and in practice to remain as close to those directives as their personal situation

---

[177] These events were composed of a cycle of sermons taking place over a period of several weeks and in an atmosphere of solemnity, preached by priests from other areas. By adapting the schedule and topics to the specific audiences, these missions were intended to permit a "return to religion" by those who had fallen away from the Church. At the end of the Mission, the parishioners were invited to a general confession.

[178] Fr. Léon Adolphe Lenfant, a priest of St. Francis de Sales, was bishop of Digne from 1915 till 1917. Originally founded by Msgr. de Ségur in 1857, Fr. Lenfant's work benefited from encouragement of the Association of St. Francis de Sales.

[179] According to Msgr. Debout, the first idea concerning this group, originally called "Society of Members of St. Francis de Sales" came in 1876. After 1890, the name was changed to the "Sons of St. Francis de Sales."

permitted. They were called by grace to this attitude of faithfulness; they professed a strong devotion to the Holy Spirit, the great sanctifier of souls. . . . The Society asked that its members be the humble auxiliaries of their parishes and of their priests. It encouraged them to join other associations that attracted their particular sense of the faith, evening adorations, third orders, brotherhoods, meetings of St. Vincent de Paul, feasts of patron saints, etc. It helped them to fulfill as best they could the obligations of the different organizations for which they might be responsible and to be useful to the clergy in every way possible.

The principal method of formation of these Sons was the observation of a Rule that required, after service to God, the fulfillment of the duties of their civil state, and the performance of certain spiritual exercises that would not be in conflict with this state. The Associates were requested as well to undertake a progressive two-year study of the doctrines of St. Francis de Sales and of the Gospels, using a method of regular exercises and questionnaires on meditations. Their spiritual progress toward the life of devotion was to be evaluated, at least on a monthly basis, when possible, through meetings with other candidates. (Msgr. Laveille)

The Society was canonically established by Cardinal Richard on March 28, 1898.[180] We can see also in the case of the Sons that no great changes in their daily

---

[180] Cardinal Lustiger recognized the Society on March 28, 2001, as a "private association of the faithful" (canons 298 ff) with a new Rule, with the title of Statutes.

lives were asked of the members. It was a question of adopting spiritual practices "to strengthen the inner man." Fr. de La Perche praised their work enthusiastically:

I found these men to be fervent Christians, whom I followed more than I directed. I tried to find for each of them the practices that were most applicable to their condition in worldly society. I saw Ernest Chaumont, the brother of the Servant of God, who was a true saint, and a few others from the group, embark resolutely on the way to Christian perfection. (Summarium)

Mlle Stiltz reported on the development of the Society in Belgium:

In Belgium the Society grew quickly. There is nothing so beautiful as to see what we call "Salesian households": father, mother, children working toward sanctification, living to love our Lord and bring others to love him, to do good together. (Summarium)

Appendix: *Probations* for the Daughters of St. Francis de Sales

In order to solicit the blessings of God for her *Probation*, the novice[181] begins her exercises on the first Friday of the month, the day that is specially dedicated to the Sacred Heart of Jesus. From then on, all the activities of her spiritual life will be directed toward the particular subject of her *Probation*. Holy

---

[181] Today we would speak of a "probanist."

Communion, the Rosary, and visiting the Blessed Sacrament will be occasions to ask God for the virtue that she must concentrate on for this month. Spiritual readings from the Gospels, St. Francis de Sales, or other authors will focus on the same subject. In a series of twelve meditations that furnish enough material to occupy all the days of the month, the novice will find a complete treatise on the nature of the virtue she is pursuing: its character, its advantages, the obstacles she might encounter, as well as the best means to acquire it, and make serious spiritual progress.

At the same time, spiritual practices help the novice not to be limited to dry theory but to exercise in her daily life the habits that strengthen the virtue on which she is concentrating. And finally, examinations of conscience adapted to her progress allow her to recognize the true dispositions of her soul with respect to each virtue, and to review all of her past with her spiritual director[182] together to prepare, better than by any other means, the resolutions she is to make at the end of the *Probation*.

The *Probations* follow a logical order and correspond to the needs of the perfect life and, specifically, of the vocation of the Daughters of St. Francis de Sales.

The first virtue is *humility.* In the spiritual life nothing serious can be pursued without the soul's knowledge and profound recognition of her nothingness before God, her misery, and the extreme need for divine grace to reach salvation and work for perfection. God sees

---

[182] Fr. Chaumont recommended the use of the "general confession."

with joy the soul sincere enough to recognize her absolute dependence on him; he is waiting only for this act of sincerity to lift the soul to the heights of faith: *Qui se humilitat exaltabitur (Who humbles himself will be exalted)*.

Once this solid foundation is in place, the novice can begin the detailed study of the perfect life. Here the three *probations* on *poverty, chastity,* and *obedience* can begin, as our Lord taught them in the Gospels and in a way that all souls seeking holiness can practice in the midst of the world.

Three other topics mark the summit of the *probations: discretion,* so necessary in the exercise of fervent faith; *gentleness and courtesy in human relations*; and perfect *docility* in her response to her spiritual director . . . thus the novice can become a precious assistant for all good works.[183]

And finally, so that these *Probations* can bring about all the good than can be hoped for, they take place over a period of time. This method allows the Daughter, who is directing the novice, the possibility of extending the trial period if the month spent on the cultivation of the virtue has not borne its full fruit. And this pause allows the novice to rest her soul and feel more ready to take advantage of the next *Probation.*[184]

Appendix: The Spirit of the Society of the Sons of St. Francis de Sales

---

[183] This topic has been replaced by "acceptance of God's will."

[184] *Notes and memories offered by the Council to Members of the Society,* 1883, quoted by Msgr. Laveille.

Its Purpose

In all walks of life we can find Christians who are filled with admiration for the ideal of holiness and feel the desire to seek the perfection of the Gospels. They have no desire to retire from the world; they have obligations here or they do not have a religious vocation. They want only to sanctify themselves as much as possible without changing their state, following Jesus Christ as closely as possible, remaining with their family, to become courageous and generous servants of the Holy Church without entering holy orders. The Society of Sons of St. Francis de Sales meets the needs of these men of good will, who sometimes cannot find support and instruction. The Society offers them the doctrine of the beautiful Saint who was destined to give future centuries the science of sanctification outside the cloister. It offers as well the counsel of priests especially prepared for this ministry. They have the benefit of meetings of mutual support that are organized so as not to interfere with the duties of their daily lives.

Methods

1) Observation of a Rule that includes exercises that can be carried out amid the demands of their usual duties.

2) Following a program of meditation and study lasting two years, in order to acquire an understanding of the teaching of St. Francis de Sales.

3) Spiritual direction once a month.

4) Meetings with other Sons to talk about their faith.

It is clear that the quality of the methods used in the Society in no way draws its members away from other good works or societies of faith of which there are many in our day. Its purpose is to provide the spiritual nourishment needed by souls seeking Christian perfection. [185]

---

[185] *Bulletin of the Priests of Saint Francis de Sales,* November 1891

CHAPTER VII

THE PRIESTS OF
SAINT FRANCIS DE SALES

The nineteenth-century clergy was very hierarchical, which meant that priests were often obliged to live alone. Many suffered from this solitude. Several bishops encouraged them to form priestly associations. Nevertheless, Fr. Chaumont's purpose in organizing his Salesian priests went beyond the goals of union and spiritual progress: The priority of the Priests of St. Francis de Sales was spiritual direction, in cooperation with the Daughters of St. Francis de Sales.

The Initial Project

Fr. Henri Chaumont was keenly aware of the difficulties faced by priests in maintaining the spirit of their mission. He spoke in the language of his time:

Many times a priest has to face the terrible temptations of Satan in order to save his soul. The life of the saintly priest of Ars was a constant struggle with the Prince of Darkness, from whose grasp he saved so many souls. The immorality surrounding the holy priest puts him to the test every day. He lives in the world, but he cannot be of the world. Even more, breathing the sickly air all around him, he must maintain a strong, vibrant spiritual life and be able to help those who are sick around him, so that they will not die, to bring back to life those who have lost their lives.[186]

At the end of 1874, as we have seen, Fr. Chaumont first thought of forming a society of Priests of St. Francis de Sales,[187] immediately receiving the encouragement of Msgr de Ségur. The initiative for this project was in fact found in Msgr. de Ségur's description of the situation of the priest, as his disciple explains:

Fortify their ministry in advance against the dangers of sadness and isolation; place their life under the protection of a saint who has been a doctor and a model for our modern times, who has provided the example of the gentlest and the strongest virtues, providing mutual support through prayer and study in order to harvest most richly the fruits of the Sacrament of Reconciliation. This is what the holy prelate hoped to see accomplished.

He wanted to avoid that priests, already overwhelmed by their active ministry, be additionally burdened with spiritual exercises. But he thought that if these exercises provided a prudent and enlightened

---

[186] Quoted by Msgr. Debout.

[187] Msgr. Laveille reported an incident that might have been at the origin of this project, one that deeply affected Fr. Chaumont, told to him by Mme Carré. A little girl died, in a rural parish, without the sacraments, due to the negligence of her local priest.

direction, the priest with deep faith would find his own sanctification and live a truly apostolic life.[188]

Msgr. de Ségur expressed these wishes for the young Society:

I wish that every day will bring you an outpouring of the Spirit of our Lord, which is contained in these two great forms of perfection and saintliness: humility and gentleness . . . courage and joy in the service of God. Let us live only for him, do good only for him, abandon ourselves, forget ourselves, to seek only the Lord and to have him reign completely in us, in place of ourselves.[189]

Fr. Chaumont drew up a preliminary Rule to distribute to the priests who might commit themselves to the Society. Shortly thereafter he wrote another, with the title of general rule, which seems less severe.[190]

The Foundation of the Society of Priests—Its Project

It became clear very quickly that Msgr. de Ségur did not have time to undertake direction of the new

---

[188] H. Chaumont, *Monseigneur de Ségur, Director of Souls.* He summarized the spirit of the Society in these words: "The motto of the family, if it had one, would be that of the Apostle: *Pax et gaudium in Spiritu Sancto.* Peace and Joy in the Holy Spirit. (*Summarium*) This is now the title of the Bulletin of the Priests of St. Francis de Sales.

[189] Letter reproduced in the *Summarium.*

[190] Since the first writing was intended for the organization of the Society of Priests of the Spirit of Jesus and the second for the Society of Priests of St. Francis de Sales, it is possible to posit the intervention of some remarks by Fr. Grandvaux.

Society, and so the task fell to Fr. Chaumont. But he could not make the decision to go ahead until he felt certain that it was indeed God's will.

He had planned to follow in the footsteps of others in the way Msgr. de Ségur had indicated, but suddenly he found himself in the position of leader. Fr. Delort came to ask advice of Fr. Chaumont. He had been the spiritual director of Sister Joseph of the Sacred Heart, a woman who had died recently and was recognized for her saintly life. Mme Carré de Malberg, for her part, begged him not to evade what she saw as a sacred duty of evangelization.

Fr. Chaumont found himself caught between the insistence of Mme Carré, who was, after all, under his spiritual direction, and his extreme hesitation born of the fear that his inadequacies would "spoil the project," as he said. It was for the glory of God that he resisted as long as possible despite the encouragement of Mme Carré. But he resolved that, if she received a sign from God or if Msgr. de Ségur put the question in the order of obedience, he would overcome his oppositions and submit immediately. (Msgr. Debout)

The Society of Priests of St. Francis de Sales was founded in 1876.[191] The members of the first council

---

[191] The first meeting of the members took place August 29, 1876, at the residence of Fr. Guéneau, first assistant of the parish of Saint-George in Paris. The following September 19, the anniversary of the apparition of La Salette, the priests began meditating on the Rule of the Society. This date was chosen as the true date of the founding. However, the "consecrations" of

were Msgr. de Ségur; Fr. Chaumont, named as the founder; Fr. Révérony of Bayeux; Fr. Delort of Aurillac; and Fr. Mienville, pastor of Bréménil. They requested approval for the Society from Msgr. Richard, archbishop coadjutor of Paris (which was obtained October 16, 1876[192]). Fr. Chaumont explained the project in these words:

This modest Society, formed on August 29, 1876, chose its title and its Rule only after submitting them to your approval, Monseigneur, and to that of Fr. Grandvaux of Saint Sulpice. Its members intend to work seriously for their own sanctification by following the lessons of St. Francis de Sales, and through extensive study of theology, in order to be useful instructors in their parishes, and effective guides in the Sacrament of Penance.[193] In order to reach these two goals:

1) *They will undertake a two-year formal spiritual formation, constant and energetic, with the intention of developing a priestly spirit, the perfect practice of Christian virtues, and zeal in seeking the salvation of souls.*

2) *They will find the theological formation necessary for the careful and fruitful administration of the sacraments in the Rule and in frequent meetings to*

---

the first three members (Frs. Chaumont, de la Perche, and Lemarchand) were not pronounced until September 19, 1878.

[192] The Society received solemn approval from Cardinal Dubois, archbishop of Paris, on January 20, 1921.

[193] It is worth noting that the letter does not mention spiritual guidance but only the Sacrament of Penance.

*study St. Thomas, St. Francis de Sales, and other
masters of the spiritual life.*

*After this long trial period, their admission to the
Society will be pronounced, but they will always
have the support of the same methods used in their
preparation to help them persevere.*[194]

*The Priests of St. Francis de Sales, even as they put
into practice the virtues leading to perfection, do not
take any external vows. If the individual confessor
thinks it prudent, he will permit private vows that
would not be communicated to the Society.*[195] *They are
and want to remain diocesan priests at the discretion
of their archbishop and all ecclesiastical superiors;
their only goal would be to imitate in all simplicity the
life of Jesus, gentle and humble of heart.*[196]

Fr. Chaumont emphasizes that the qualities of these
priests should be above average. He reminds us that
the judgment of God will be harsher for the priest: *"He
must not be content to be only correct, organized, and
conventional in his faith and devotion. God expects*

---

[194] Fr. Chaumont indicates here that even after reception into
the Society, the priests will follow *probations.*

[195] The Rule encouraged the priests of the Society to cultivate
the virtues of poverty, chastity, and obedience, but it did not ask
for a public profession of these virtues, as members of religious
congregations do. Fr. Chaumont reaffirms that the priests of St.
Francis remain diocesan priests, subject to the authority of their
bishop. He wanted to reassure bishops that the priests of the
Society would not escape their authority.

[196] Quoted by Msgr. Debout.

something quite different from those to whom his Son has entrusted this priesthood." (Msgr. Debout)

He [Chaumont] wrote a questionnaire concerning priests who were asking for admission to the Society, to evaluate their precise qualities:

1) *In the seminary, was he an example of assiduity and devotion?*

2) *Is he now respected and considered to be sincere in his diocese?*

3) *Do you think he is sincere in his desire to sanctify himself and develop his inner life?*

4) *Is his judgment sure and reflective?*

5) *Does he care fervently for the salvation and sanctification of souls?*

6) *Does he have, or do you see that he is capable of developing, a character that is gentle, conciliatory, and generous?*

7) *Does he have an irreproachable attitude toward diocesan authority?*

8) *Does he know about the Society? Has he shown his desire to enter it?*

9) *Will he know the methods of St. Francis de Sales well enough to use them in the direction of souls?*[197]

---

[197] Letter of September 1881, quoted by Msgr. Debout.

Starting with the retreat he preached to the Society in 1892, Fr. Chaumont enumerated the qualities these priests should seek: humility, in the image of Jesus Christ; simplicity;[198] and generosity, *"because the life of Jesus was an act of love for his father."*[199] He invited them to always keep before them the perspective of death and salvation, not making this earthy life the final goal. Their appearance should always express *"modest dignity and a welcoming friendliness."* [200] Remembering the cheerful nature of St. Francis de Sales,[201] he nevertheless did not dwell on it, preferring to encourage the priests to read Holy Scripture and maintain their priestly demeanor. He insisted especially on the aptitudes they should cultivate in administering the Sacrament of Penance and

---

[198] "Simplicity is the order and harmony that arrange all intentions so well that they become a single intention. Everything is unified in the love of God. . . . [The pure soul] sees the things of this world but moves beyond them; it brings everything to the glory of God. The rest is merely stones on the road; the eyes see them but do not look purposefully at them." H. Chaumont, *Memories of the Retreat of Athis. A Secretary's Notes.* 1892

[199] H. Chaumont, *Memories of the Retreat of Athis.*

[200] H. Chaumont, *Memories of the Retreat of Athis.* He had some difficulty clearly defining his terms here. He wants a mixture of goodness and simplicity that go far beyond worldly courtesy.

[201] "I do not reproach this lovable cheerfulness, these good spirits that our Saint called *eutrapélie.*" He himself loved not only smiling but also making those around him laugh. Nevertheless, St. Francis de Sales was extremely careful of his language. He retained from his extensive early reading of profane authors only what could serve God and the salvation of souls. H. Chaumont, *Memories of the Retreat of Athis.*

especially in dealing with people who frequently accused themselves of venial sins:

A priest becomes accustomed to treating venial sins lightly, since he has heard so many crimes. What will be God's judgment of us if these negligences are never addressed or combatted or corrected, and what will God have in store for the priest who cares so little about pleasing him?[202]

On the same theme in preaching a retreat, he painted a dark picture of the parish under the guidance of a negligent priest:

He spouts heresies as if they were water; he grants all dispensations; confers the Sacrament of Penance without explanations, without questions, offering no counsel. [203]

It is impossible to imagine a Priest of St. Francis de Sales who understands his vocation, who is trying to become the perfect director of souls, who, once he has given absolution leaves the process there, saying, "That's good enough, sufficient. He should give of

---

[202] Minutes of the meetings of October 3 and 17, 1888, quoted by Msgr. Debout.

[203] The retreat of 1888 at Nevers, quoted by Msgr. Debout. Fr. Chaumont was speaking here in the language of Alphonsus Ligouri, who asked that priests give "medicinal penances" intended to cure the habit that draws one to sin, and requires that the priest ask questions in confession that will allow him to give helpful guidance to the soul.

himself, not only to some, but to all, not up to a certain point, but totally.[204]

He warned against "worldly priests." He did not limit his criticism to admonitions given to members of the Society; he spoke in a similar vein to the parishioners of Sainte Clotilde during Lent of 1869 and 1870. He gave them this advice concerning their relationship with their priests: *"Be on your guard; listen to what they say but do not imitate them and do not entrust your soul to them."* (Msgr. Debout) He foresaw that some members of the Society would not be faithful to the standards he set; thus, he provided that they could be temporarily excluded from the group and placed in a sort of "infirmary," where they could be helped by their brothers in the Society until they had recovered their discipline and appropriate relations with their vocation. He added encouraging words:

Let us not forget that as priests we are the dearest, favored disciples of Jesus; that the mission he has confided to us assures us of beautiful rights in his spiritual kingdom, and that consequently we have an infinite reservoir of pardon and strength to compensate for our weaknesses. [205]

Fr. Chaumont emphasized the importance of a prayer life, even for priests who are very busy, and invited his priests not to see an opposition between prayer and action:

---

[204]*Retreat of Athis,* quoted by Msgr. Debout.
[205] Letter of Fr. Chaumont, November 12, 1877, quoted by Msgr. Debout.

One of the great shortcomings of our nature is to have a too limited and exclusive view of our possibilities. A person who is passionate in the desire for evangelization may give second place in life to the essential, that is, the life of constant prayer; another who has tasted how sweet and gentle God's ways are may neglect duties toward fellow human beings, who are so often inconsistent and tiresome.

Jesus, the eternal model of the priest, had a clearer vision. Everything he did for the salvation of souls was intended for the glory of his Heavenly Father, and at the same time his passion and devotion to his father never interfered with his ministry to the neediest souls. . . . And so, Father, do not be content to lament at the feet of Jesus, about how our Lord is abandoned in the churches. Think of ingenious ways to awaken in the excellent priests around you the thought to come more often to the tabernacle and to attract their parishioners to meet them there.[206]

He explained that caring for souls was the essential way for a priest to reach his own sanctification. This was close to the declaration made during Vatican II, *"For priests, the authentic path to saintliness is through the loyal and tireless exercise of their functions in the Spirit of Christ."* [207] Indeed, Fr. Chaumont wrote:

---

[206] Letter of Fr. Chaumont to Fr. Landon, August 8, 1882, quoted by Msgr. Debout.
[207] Vatican II, Decree on the Ministry and the Life of Priests, *Presbyterorum Ordinis,* number 13.

170

You have a thousand reasons to be vigilant that nothing created comes between you and Jesus, even on the pretext that it is part of your ministry.[208] *Only what is pure is worthy of love, only what is in Jesus is completely pure. Jesus is everything, the principle, the means and the end. But all of this must be kept safe in the life of prayer, by serious mortification, by worthy respect for the sacraments, and fully spiritual celebration of the Holy Mass. It is certain that caring for souls is not an obstacle to the personal sanctification of the priest called to the apostolic ministry. It is one of the most precious means to sanctification and a very sure one. The concern for souls can never be too great nor our devotion to their salvation excessive. We are the instruments of the Lord's grace. . . . Jesus wants to use our unworthy hands to distribute his most precious gifts. The priest who consecrates and absolves is making as much progress in saintliness and perfection as when he distributes the sacred Bread and God's pardon. Jesus will never permit, no, never, that the priest, detached from everything and from himself, for Jesus's sake, in order to live completely for others' souls, be less united with Jesus or that he love Jesus less when he loves souls through him, in him, in his adorable generosity.*[209]

---

[208] In the following lines it becomes clear that Fr. Chaumont was not inviting the priests to neglect their duties toward the souls entrusted to them. It was because they have put Jesus first in their lives and maintain such a close relationship with him that they can be useful in their mission.

[209] Letter from Fr. Chaumont to Fr. Landon, September 7, 1882, quoted by Msgr. Debout.

Fr. Chaumont explained clearly to his new recruits who already had a spiritual director that there would be no rivalry between the two:

It is agreed between us, dear brother in Christ, that your director of conscience, far from losing any rights over you, gains one more, that of monitoring the counsels that will be given to you through the Society. But on the other hand, he will need to support you in this undertaking. (Summarium)

The Probation Method

As the priest explained in the retreat he preached to the priests of the Society in 1892, in order to imitate Christ in the footsteps of St. Francis de Sales, they should have no other guide than the "Spirit of Jesus."

Your point of departure should be: From now on, I should no longer embody the human spirit except insofar as it is not in contradiction to the Holy Spirit; I will be wise, but with the wisdom of God. I will seek happiness but the happiness of heaven. I want to appreciate the things of this world only as I appreciate them in the Lord. I will be inspired in all things by the Holy Spirit. Before each of my actions, I will ask myself, "Is this what the Holy Spirit would ask for?" I will take my inspiration only from that source.[210]

In order to reach this goal, Fr. Chaumont used the method of *Probations* that he had originally put in place for the Daughters, adapting it to the Society of Priests.

---

[210] Henri Chaumont, *Memoirs of the Retreat of Athis.*

For an entire month, the priest will devote himself to the study of a special virtue. He must concentrate his meditations, his prayers, all of his efforts toward this goal. Specific directives help guide him in this task. At the end of the month, using a questionnaire developed for this purpose, he must review in his mind the spiritual work he has accomplished, note his constancy or his failures, determine how to correct any weaknesses, and find suitable remedies and resolutions to adopt in order to reach his goal. This is his chance to examine the state of his soul, . . . in relation to the priestly ideal, to determine if he is approaching this goal successfully, or with insufficient fervor. The questionnaire will be sent at the beginning of each month to the probateur, who returns it to his protégé with written comments, advice, or useful encouragements. (Msgr. Debout)

The *Probations* follow a predetermined order: Those dealing with humility, poverty, chastity, and obedience are intended to lead one toward "letting go," and those concentrating on the Blessed Sacrament and the direction of souls are aimed at "renewing and beautifying the soul." [211] Just as in the case of the Daughters, where the *Probatrices* were responsible for the preparation of new members, the *Probateurs* had a parallel role vis-à-vis the priests. The director of the *Probateurs* described their qualities:

---

[211] Henri Chaumont, *Memoir of the Retreat of Athis.* Three other probations were added: the imitation of St. Francis de Sales and devotion to the blessed Virgin and to the Church and the Holy See.

He must be beyond reproach, . . . filled with practical wisdom, fair, saintly; no lesson from the lips of such a priest should astonish; no admonition should lead to bitterness; no demand should seem excessive. If he is young, the quality of his life should be such that his age is of no consequence; he must be unfailingly devout. Spiritual paternity, on whatever person it is exercised, requires a great degree of self-abnegation.

The probateur must have zeal and a capacity for emulation that refuses no sacrifice; he must help his brothers to withstand their difficult times and take advantage of their moments of fervor; he must support them when they are weak and keep them from falling during those bad days from which the disciple will go forth strengthened. His heart will be less attached to all that is human and more attached to things celestial, more fully a priest, more an apostle.[212]

The correspondence between Cardinal Tisserant and his *Probateur,* recently analysed by Hervé Gaignard, shows how the disciple was led to a life in faith that was adapted not only to the work he might be doing[213] but also to his temperament, which he was encouraged to see as an "expression of divine providence" intended to accomplish the task at hand.[214] On several

---

[212] Quoted by Msgr. Debout. He explained that after the General Chapter meeting of the Society, which took place at Paray-Le-Monial in 1893, the Directory was established. This document no longer exists. The text can still be found in the *Handbook of Probateurs* in use today.

[213] At the time he entered the Society, he was working in the manuscript department of the Vatican Library.

[214] Hervé Gaignard, *The Spiritual Life of Cardinal Eugene Tisserant: Between Perfection and Sainthood (1908–1945)*, Paris,

occasions, his *Probateur*[215] helped him to overcome spiritual crises, by counselling him to practice prudence and perseverance and helping him to see the ambiguities of his attitudes.

The Expansion of the Society

In Paris, Fr. Chaumont had the advantage of the support of Msgr. Richard, archbishop-coadjutor. In other areas he was less well known and he thought it wise not to intervene directly. He did not want to give the appearance of being a moral authority in competition with the bishop of other dioceses through his relationship with the local priests. He decided, for example, that the group in Lyon, founded in 1881, should be independent under the authority of Frs. Bonnardet and Nugue. The decision was made never to publish a list of members outside of the Society itself, except in the case of bishops who wanted to see it. For the same reason, Fr. Chaumont waited for three years before he wrote to the archbishop of Rheims, Cardinal Langénieux, on the subject of the group of priests in his diocese. In the same spirit, Fr. Chaumont wanted to know what positions priests who wanted to enter the Society held.

The motive for this last question is to protect our little Society from any suspicion that might harm it. In similar societies, if a member is affiliated with the

Parole and Silence. Toulouse, Center of History and Theology, 2009.
[215] It was Charles Ruch (1873–1945), professor of dogma at the major seminary of Nancy, and future bishop of Strasbourg.

diocesan administration, there may be hostile minds that suspect interference of that society in the administration. However, that is completely opposed to our principles. We would have difficulty admitting into our Society a priest who is involved in diocesan administration.[216]

Relations were established between the Society of Priests of St. Francis de Sales and the Apostolic Union of Clergy: [217]

On December 26, 1881, the Society of Priests of St. Francis de Sales was officially affiliated with the Apostolic Union. . . . Fr. Chaumont hoped that it would bring word of his Society to more priests and extend the good that he wanted to do. . . . This affiliation, which became nearly a unification of the two societies on a few points, lasted until the dimensions of the two obliged them to separate; nevertheless, they remained attached by the bonds of strong friendship. (Msgr. Debout)

The two societies agreed that priests belonging to the Union could join the Society of St. Francis de Sales without losing their membership in the former organization. Fr. Chaumont pointed out this difference

---

[216] Letter by Chaumont, September 20, 1881, quoted by Msgr. Debout.
[217] The Union was founded in 1868 by a director of the seminary of Orleans, the Sulpician Victor Lebeurier, to counter the isolation of priests. At present this organization sponsors a session of spirituality every three years and offers to its members a review titled *Diocesan Priests.*

between the Society of St. Francis de Sales and other associations of priests:

Our Society, although it resembles other priestly societies that seek to maintain their members in the habits of devotion that they learned in Seminary, is different in that our goal is especially the sanctification of the souls entrusted to each priest. For our sister societies, this goal is secondary to seeking the sanctification of the priest himself. Whereas the other societies leave this quest to the initiative of the individual priest, our Society guides him through a structure prepared in advance, according to the spirit of St. Francis de Sales. (Msgr. Debout)

Coordination of the Society of Priests took place through meetings of the group in Paris under the leadership of Fr. Chaumont:

These meetings at first took place every two weeks and lasted an hour and a quarter. The first fifteen minutes were devoted to reading minutes and hearing news of the Society; then came the study of St. Francis de Sales; thirdly, an exhortation by the spiritual father, followed by "mea culpas," and the final quarter hour was devoted to discussion of a particular case of conscience. To be exact, this order of events was adopted in the summer of 1882; originally Fr. Chaumont's exhortation took up most of the time. It is significant that he is called the Spiritual Father. It was he who did not want to be called president or director general, thus the title by which he was known. (Msgr. Debout)

In fact, since Fr. Chaumont refused to be the superior general of the Society, at his death the Society was directed by a general council, which from time to time was opened to representatives of the groups. It thus became a *Chapter*[218] and exercised plenary powers over the Society.[219] The circulars insist on the need for punctuality at meetings and specify that the last part of the meetings be devoted to the *mea culpas.*[220] On this point Fr. Chaumont explained that it was best to be truthful, even if it is unpleasant to hear:

Goodness, which is the key to the method of St. Francis de Sales does not consist in closing our eyes to the imperfections of his disciples, nor in being content with them in a minimum of Christian life. On the contrary, it is a skilful construction by which we first gain their hearts. Then we dare to ask from them total renunciation of their own will, a love of God beyond measure, and regarding our fellow humans, a devotion for which no sacrifice is too much.[221]

---

[218] Today we would say general assembly.

[219] Nevertheless, in the first years of the twentieth century a few difficulties appeared, arising from the fear of overlapping authority between the spiritual father in Paris and the *Probateur General.* At a *Chapter* held in Ars, in July 1920, the decision was made that the Society would be presided over by a general director with the help of and under the control of the general council and the *Chapter.*

[220] Today the expression "review of life" is the usual term (relating one's failures).

[221] Text quoted by Msgr. Debout. We note that this admonition was applied equally to the Society of Priests and to the Daughters of St. Francis de Sales.

Fr. Chaumont sent a message, including his Christmas greetings, to all the priests of the Society in December of each year. He also sent greetings for saints' days and birthdays to his fellow priests, and asked them to send their photographs, which he compiled in albums of twenty, to be given to the different groups in an effort to make them acquainted with one another.[222]

The First Retreats

Brother Joseph, superior of the Brothers of Christian Doctrine, offered the house d'Athis, near Paris for the first retreat of the Priests of St. Francis de Sales, September 20–24, 1886.[223] Fr. Joseph Tissot, superior general of the Missionaries of St. Francis de Sales of Annecy, preached the retreat. Many priests attended. In the message that Fr. Chaumont addressed to the members of the Society after the event, he recalled the high points of the experience:

[Fr. Tissot] had barely had time to leave his luggage in his room before a priest asked him to decide the question of his vocation. If Fr. Tissot said the word, this new brother would be one of us and join in our spiritual exercises. If not, he would be obliged to give up this wonderful dream and catch the next train in order to make his retreat somewhere else starting the next morning. The interview was brief. Very soon Fr.

---

[222] The method seems quite usual to us today. Starting at that time there were albums assembling a number of photographs but they were usually made up of famous people.

[223] Retreats for men began to develop during the 1880s. This house was one of the places open for such a purpose in the Paris region.

Tissot brought the new candidate to us, with triumphant joy: "Take him; I am sure of his vocation." These words worked a magical transformation. The rather aloof priest who had seemed all urbanity, a bit solemn, became a friendly, simple, and charming brother. An hour later it seemed that he had always been a member of the Society.

Right after dinner, our guest preacher gave us the topic for our prayers for the next day; we all entered into the spirit of reflection he had suggested and remained in that state of mind even during our recreation periods. At the same time, as we followed the useful courses of instruction, we attended meetings concerning the Society. . . . The further we advanced in the exercises of the retreat, the more we felt bonded in love, according to the true apostolic spirit, a single soul and a single heart. Before we ended, in the presence of the Holy Sacrament exposed in front of us, three new brothers made their professions,[224] with the support of forty priests of St. Francis de Sales.[225]

Msgr. Debout added his memories of the founder to this report of the retreat:

During recreation times he greeted everyone, welcoming the opportunity to walk with anyone who asked for that privilege; answering requests and trying to anticipate, in the eyes of the most timid the questions that they were afraid to ask. During the entire recreation he was at our disposition, receiving all, and

---

[224] They were received as full-fledged members of the Society.
[225] Circular letter from Fr. Chaumont October 1, 1886, quoted by Msgr. Debout.

arranging to give the necessary time to those who had more serious questions to discuss. In his responses, he was both firm and gentle; his expression could plead and command, but never lose the sense of constant and unalterable peace. When the bell rang to end our recreation and bring us back to our classrooms, he rose without seeming too rushed or too indifferent. He went to the little chapel used for our lectures, walking in silence unless he felt obliged to respond in a low voice to the request of a fellow priest too anxious to wait for a later opportunity to speak to him.

At meals he remained plunged into his reflections, looking neither to the left nor to the right. Nevertheless he was always attentive to the needs of those seated next to him at the table, making sure that they had all they needed. (Msgr. Debout)

Msgr. Debout told how, at the same retreat, Fr. Chaumont convinced the members to give up calling him by the title of "superior general" of the Society:[226]

The second retreat of the Priests of St. Francis de Sales opened on July 21, 1889, at Athis-Mons. Fr. Guéneau, who was at that time assigned to Saint Nicholas du Chardonnet, preached the retreat, with the assistance of Fr. Paillet, Fr. Chaumont's secretary. At that time the members were able to congratulate the founder

---

[226] It was clear that Fr. Chaumont played this role. Nevertheless, he refused to use the title, alleging a number of reasons that Msgr. Debout did not mention. But we can surmise that the founder was sensitive to the question of how some of the bishops might interpret this initiative, reading into the title a diminution of their hierarchical authority.

being named a canon. Fr. Chaumont himself preached the following retreat in 1892. This was his outline:

First Day

- Opening, the graces of the retreat
- First instruction: on the spirit of the Society
- First lesson: St. Francis de Sales

Second Day

- Meditation, spiritual identity of a Priest of St. Francis de Sales
- Second instruction: from the founding of a Society of Priests in the school of St. Francis de Sales. Conversion of the will.

- Third instruction: on the spiritual identity of a Priest of St. Francis de Sales

Third Day

- Meditation, the present life
- Fourth instruction: conduct and attitudes of a Priest of St. Francis de Sales
- Conversation: caution on the part of the priest in his relationships with souls
- Fifth instruction: the priests of St. Francis de Sales as directors of souls

Fourth Day

- Meditation, the judgments of men and the judgments of God; salvation.

- Sixth instruction: evangelizing by the Priest of St. Francis de Sales

- Conversation: resolutions to be taken

- Seventh instruction: auxiliaries of the Priests of St. Francis de Sales

- Eighth instruction: the future of the priests of the Society

Meditation, gratitude

The Society had thirty-two members in 1877 and nearly 100 by December 1882. There were 152 at the end of October 1884.[227] The Society grew quickly during those years: 765 in 1895; 1,102 in 1898 (639 members and 463 in formation); 2,078 in 1926 (1,400 members and 678 in formation).

Today, the Society of the Priests of St. Francis de Sales has spread throughout the world.[228]

Appendix: The Rule of the Society of Priests of Saint Francis de Sales

---

[227] That was the time when the number of diocesan priests in France reached the highest number, 55,000, between 1890 and 1905.

[228] Europe (France, Belgium, Poland, Switzerland); Africa (Benin, Burkina Faso, Cameroon, Central Africa, Democratic Republic of the Congo, Côte d'Ivoire, Nigeria, Rwanda, Senegal, Tanzania, Togo); Indian Ocean (Madagascar, Île Maurice); the Americas (Argentina, Brazil, Colombia, Haiti, Chile); Asia (Bangladesh, India, Sri Lanka, Indonesia).

Its Purpose

The Society of the Spirit of Jesus[229] does not propose directly to facilitate the exercise of devotion and fervor among priests in their duties in this sacred ministry. The Church, through the voice of the Council of Trent, the writings and examples of St. Charles Borromeo,[230] and many others, continues to remind them of the overwhelming responsibilities of their vocation.

We have a very special purpose. The priests in our Society want to fully live in the spirit of Our Lord and to communicate this spirit to the souls in their charge. They seek, in the complete meaning of the words, to become Jesus for their flock.[231] To reach this goal, they promise to observe the following rules concerning the practice of their special vocation as directors and their relationships with each other:

Rules Concerning Spiritual Direction

In order to live constantly in the Spirit of our Lord Jesus and to become truly Jesus for these souls, these priests seek perfection *for* spiritual direction, *in* spiritual direction, and *by* spiritual direction.

---

[229] As the *Summarium* indicated, this was the original title that Fr. Chaumont wanted to give the Society. He modified this on the advice of Msgrs. Granvaux and Richard.

[230] Saint Charles Borromeo (1538–1584 archbishop of Milan, was a model for the clergy following the Council of Trent. After his death, some of his writings were collected in *The Pastoral of Saint Charles*, which was a veritable guide for pastors for many centuries.

[231] The expression is taken directly from Msgr. de Ségur.

1. How they should prepare themselves to be a spiritual director

The great ministry of the direction of souls (*ars artium*)[232] requires twofold preparation in the priests who exercise it: one for the spirit, the other for the heart. For the spirit, they must have true knowledge of God and of souls. For the heart, they need true saintliness in the spirit of Jesus.

A. Acquiring knowledge of God and of souls

The study of theology, either elementary or abstract, cannot be sufficient for priests called to spiritual direction. Such priests must have the special science that St. Paul called simply "*Jesus Christum et hunc crucifixum*"[233] (1 Cor. 2:2), because outside of Jesus everything is truly nothingness; Jesus is the only Master, the only savior, the only "consumer" of all our life.[234] They must study all of the virtues found *in* Jesus: renunciation, humility, goodness, love, devotion; they will not understand all of these great things unless they have reflected often on them before the tabernacle or at the feet of Christ Crucified. [235]

B. To the study of Jesus they should add the study of souls . . .

---

[232] This expression, "the art of arts," comes from Gregory the Great (*Pastoral Rule, first part, chapter I*). It expresses how spiritual direction should take first place in priestly ministry.

[233] Jesus Christ and Jesus Christ crucified.

[234] That is, "he who brings our life to its consummation, its fulfilment."

[235] Fr. Chaumont is referring here to the work by Msgr. Charles Gay, *Concerning Christian Virtues.*

Called to become the father of souls, the spiritual director should know, like St. Paul, that he will give birth to them in pain; he must learn all of the means to help them to grow in Jesus and to lead them to the fullness of the perfect human being.

Called to become the doctor of souls, he must know in advance all of their weaknesses, their infirmities; thus he should know as well the healing offered by the grace of Jesus, and the experience of the saints.

Called to be their judge, he must know not all the reasons he might have to condemn them; on the contrary, he must be aware of all the resources given to us by God's mercy that can deflect harsh justice and bring pardon.[236]

To acquire this knowledge, of Jesus and of souls, the priest will need to know as fully as possible:

a) The most important book, the Holy Scriptures, the New Testament, and in the New Testament, the Gospel of John, which St. Philip Néri, the great confessor, director, and sanctifier of souls read and reread as his only text through his old age.

b) The lives of saints, which constitute true practical and theoretical commentaries on the life of Jesus. He should study especially the saintly directors such as St. Francis de Sales and the lives of the

---

[236] Fr. Chaumont reviews the list of qualities that a confessor should possess, as found in detail in works from that period. It is clear that his vision is far removed from the spirit of Jansenism and the rigors that it fostered.

saints who can serve as models for the Christians whose spiritual life he will be guiding.

c) Works of theology, true dogmatic theology, that are necessary in order to understand the place of Jesus in all things; texts not to be confused with the countless works using this title but that are in fact just polemic tracts; true morality not inspired by rigors akin to Jansenism, or an arbitrary perspective that opens the door to every abuse, but the morality that the Roman Catholic Church recommends in her official teaching; and finally, the true sense of mystery that draws everything to Jesus, the practical science of mysteries midway between dry metaphysics that only speak to the intellect and books of popular piety full of sentiments but no doctrine, ubiquitous today.[237]

2. *Asking for saintliness in the spirit of Jesus*

Since the director has to be Jesus for souls, he must try with all his strength to become a saint.

In order to do this, the Spirit of our Savior must penetrate him completely. Thus the priests who are members of this Society must apply themselves to living completely in Jesus Christ, practicing the great rule of Gospel perfection: *manete in me et ego in*

---

[237] Fr. Chaumont did not hesitate to state his position: on the one hand against dry scholasticism, against Jansenism and rigors, against laxity which left all decisions in the hands of the confessor (a subjective morality), but also against a sentimental, watered-down spirituality that was a speciality of the nineteenth century.

vobis.[238] From this determination will flow a powerful spirit of prayer that will envelop them and penetrate them, everywhere and always, keeping them fully immersed in Christ. They will never, through their own fault, leave this unity.

They will possess a pure light of faith that will make the mysterious secrets of Jesus intelligible for them: love for human souls, a deep respect for the Sovereign Pontiff, Vicar of Christ, and Doctor of Truth. [239]

They will possess an immense love for the Blessed Sacrament and the Holy Virgin.

They will possess fervor for mortification, maintaining the body in servitude and transforming it *in novitate spiritus.*[240]

In Jesus, these priests will find the humility of adoration and of prayer; the humility of confusion, contrition and penitence.[241]

In Jesus they will find the strong and kind gentleness that will provide the inner peace that can radiate to all

---

[238] "Abide in me and I in you." (John 15:4)

[239] Note the importance of the pope in the years following Vatican Council I.

[240] "In a renovation of spirit" or "according to a renewed spirit." A negative view of the body, as opposed to the spirit, is noticeable here.

[241] This image of a humble Jesus adoring the Father is inherited from the French school of spirituality.

of their relationships with God and with their fellow human beings.[242]

In Jesus, with Jesus, and like Jesus they will celebrate the Holy Sacrifice, identifying so completely with him that they will receive from God, for themselves and for the souls confided to them, all the desired graces of sanctification.

They will practice poverty, like Jesus, and in Jesus, holding on to nothing on this earth and living in great simplicity.[243] They will practice holy chastity like Jesus, and in Jesus, with infinite discretion, especially in the confessional, and in their relationships with those they guide. They will practice with Jesus, and in Jesus, holy obedience, making God's will their constant rule of conduct, their nourishment, and their life.[244]

In summary, they will do everything, as far as human weakness allows, with the saintliness and in the saintliness of Jesus, trying to be Jesus in all things, within and without, in relation to God and to their neighbor. Consequently, they will love neither this world nor its practices. When they are obliged to

---

[242] Here we find the heritage of St. Francis de Sales.

[243] We notice here Fr. Chaumont's intuition, which began with the *Association of Saint-Sulpice,* during his years in the seminary.

[244] Fr. Chaumont enumerates the evangelical counsels. The priests are not called to make solemn vows, like members of a religious congregation, but to live constantly with these considerations. Fr. Chaumont's concern for chastity and especially prudence in the confessional is manifest in these admonitions. He personally refused any kind of familiarity with women.

participate in it, they will do so with modest dignity, with reserve mixed with friendliness, in a manner that recalls for all, Jesus, gentle and humble of heart. And finally they will take special care not to confuse their sacred ministry with considerations of material ambition or gain.[245]

II. How the Priests should become Jesus in spiritual direction

Intellectual preparation and the search for holiness are not enough for spiritual direction to produce all the good fruits of salvation that God intends. Two other conditions are indispensable in the practice of this difficult mission. The Spirit of God reveals them to us by his example: *attingit a fine usque ad finem fortiter et disponit omnia suaviter;* [246] *Fortitur* in the direction of souls means energy and caution; *suaviter* means gentleness and love.

1. Never forget to exercise the prudence of God

The Priests of the Society will never forget the rules of prudence required by their vocation.

This ministry absorbs all of their lives, leaving scarcely enough time to pray, to meditate, and to study. It requires them to do all for everyone, in order to win them to Jesus Christ, to know their sorrows, their temptations, and their failures. It is a responsibility

---

[245] Here the priest is warning against becoming a "priest in elegant society," the notion of "worldly sin" taken from John's gospel, when he warns against these temptations.

[246] The spirit extends with strength from one end of the earth to the other and it does all things with gentleness. (Wisdom, 8:1)

that seemed overwhelming to St. Vincent de Paul. On the other hand, the exceptional confidence that is accorded to them, the indications of veneration that they receive and cannot avoid noticing, the awareness, though blameless, of the progress made by the souls he leads, constitute another danger that we sometimes are not enough aware of, that could entail great dangers and erase that special grace that comes from spiritual direction.

Thus the priests of this Society are committed to observe the rules of holy prudence in all areas.

They will not hide the truth; they will speak clearly of God's rights, and they will not try to limit delicate questions of conscience. They will remember that one characteristic of the Sovereign Sanctifier of souls is to teach the whole truth, to teach the souls entrusted to him the practice of everything that Jesus commanded, to detach them from everything that is not in search of their salvation.

They will remember that they did not choose the ministry that they exercise but that God has chosen them for this holy vocation. When they see the abundant fruits of their labors, they will remember that all the honor belongs to God. . . .

Above all they will observe at all times extreme reserve, never breaking the strict rule, applied firmly, *noli me tangere.*[247] Their language will always be

---

[247] "Do not touch me." (John 20:17) Fr. Chaumont applied this rule at all times and in every way in his life.

worthy of Jesus, avoiding any affected or affectionate terms that are not appropriate for their ministry. . . .

2. *Revealing the ineffable goodness of Our Lord.*

Prudence, if it were the only quality in the director, would make him seem harsh; prudence must give way also to gentleness: *a fine ad finem fortite* meets *omnia suaviter.* The priest director must be good with the goodness of Jesus himself. He must never frighten anyone; he must be solicitous of all but especially toward the humble, the poor, the least of our brethren.

If he has any favorites, they are among the sinners, and for those who suffer. If he exhausts himself, it is in search of the lost lamb.

He has a word of pardon for all, for Magdalene, for the woman taken in adultery, for Peter, for the thief.

He must never bring false severity to his doctrines that would make the yoke and the burden heavy that should be light and easy.

He must be patient, forgiving not seven times but seventy times seven, the sorrow that these souls cause him. He will never despair of any of them, no matter how guilty or how obstinate they may continue to be.

He will always be available, never complaining that his children bother their father, giving each one, whether it is convenient or not, the encouragement of a kind word, the light of wise advice, or strength and joy.

He will try not to fall into the shortcomings that are natural to us all: being rushed,[248] lacking in good manners, or ridiculing. These are practices that could alienate or make those uncomfortable who come to him for guidance.

He will recommend devotion to the Holy Virgin, so that they become accustomed to turning to this good and tender Mother.

Above all, his ministry should initiate his people, whoever they may be, to knowledge and love of the Eucharist. All holiness and perfection are united in it; it is the beginning and the end. Nothing can take its place; the Eucharist is everything, because it is Jesus.

III.   How they will be able to gain the full fruits of spiritual direction.
As the stream that flows through sweetness is perfumed, the director who is a channel of grace for souls, giving everything that he receives, nevertheless conserves everything that he gives. It all becomes precious graces for his sanctification. The priests of the Spirit of Jesus will be sanctified by their spiritual direction.

1.   Gaining from what they say to others.
The priests of this Society will try to give up everything in the exercise of the direction of souls, letting the Spirit of Our Savior speak in them and through them, learning from the lessons they give to others.

---

[248] Fr. Chaumont was speaking here of a priest who would be in a rush to end a confession.

2.   *Gaining from what they hear.*[249]

In every conscience, even the least awakened, there is a trace of the work of the Holy Spirit. The light that an important question can shine into a soul can bring about a remarkable response. If Mary found much to meditate on in the conversation of the shepherds surrounding the manger, then surely many times in a single day spent in the service of souls, the spiritual director may find precious lights that are abundant subjects for meditation!

There is more: When the priest moves beyond the limits of a simple confession to the area of serious spiritual direction, he becomes part of encouraging works of grace. He notices such progress in virtue, sees the words of the prophet brought to life—*sicut gigas ad currendam viam suam*[250]—that he hardly knows how to feel humble enough in the face of his own failings, and he makes great resolutions to be able to follow those he is supposed to lead.

Thus, Jesus, who is truly all in all, consumes them both in the same Spirit and the same love, before he rewards them both in the same glory.

Rules concerning the relationship of the Priests of the Spirit of Jesus among themselves

The Society has chosen Msgr. de Ségur for its Spiritual Father.

---

[249] It is significant that Fr. Chaumont explains that the director can also receive from those he directs.
[250] [He has lunged forward] like a giant running to arrive at his destination. (Ps 19(18):6) [Is (18) correct?]

It is directed by a Council that will meet every Monday.

The members of the Society promise:
1. To devote themselves as much as is possible to the direction of souls.

2. To have and to observe a *rule of life as approved by the Spiritual Father or their confessor.*

This rule will include:

3. Some acts of mortification every day, for the souls in their care, the monthly retreat, the first Friday. On that day, they will offer a secondary Mass intention for all the priests of the Society, and read the Rule of the Society.
4. Attend a major retreat every year, before which the priest will consult the Spiritual Father or, with his permission, another member of the Society.

5. Write a report every three months to the Spiritual Father covering observation of the Rule.

6. Never leave a letter unanswered from a member priest asking for advice concerning the direction of souls.

Admitting priests to the Society

1. Any priest who promises to observe the conditions mentioned above may become a member of the Society.

2. He will be presented to the Council and must be accepted by all of the members.

3. If he is already a priest, preparation of only one year will be required of him.

4. If he is not yet a priest, he will be received at the time of his ordination, provided that he has served at least one year in the apostolate.

5. During his preparation, he will write every two months to the Spiritual Father or to the priest that he will have named to replace him, to report on his progress in the exercise of the special virtues of a minister of direction.

6. If the priest is accepted by the Council, he will make his consecration according to the forms that will be described further on.

A priest who is living at a distance from all other members of the Society will make his consecration by celebrating the holy Mass for his own intention on a day that will be decided for him.[251]

---

[251] The Rule reproduced here is by Msgr. Debout.

CHAPTER VIII

FATHER CHAUMONT—HIS MINISTRY

We left the story of Fr. Chaumont at the end of his years as an assistant at Sainte Clotilde. As we return to his life now, he is no longer the young priest whose reserve and discernment were so appreciated at the beginning of his ministry. He has become a widely recognized spiritual figure, the founder of several societies and, in spite of his humility, known by his disciples as "our reverend father."

Chaplain for the Christian Brothers

The congregation of Christian Brothers, founded in 1681 by Jean-Baptiste de la Salle (1651–1719)[252] underwent a rapid renaissance after the [French] Revolution.[253]

The motherhouse on the rue Oudinot included 300 men in 1854, and 500 twenty years later. Fr. Chaumont became principal chaplain following the departure of Fr. Roche, who was named bishop of Gap. The residents included Brothers responsible for the central administration, the major novitiate and the preparatory

---

[252] Jean-Baptiste de la Salle was canonized May 24, 1900, and named patron of educators May 15, 1950.

[253] In 1854, the congregation included 730 schools throughout the world and 5,670 members; in 1878, there were more than 2,100 communities worldwide, 1,800 in France, 46 in the colonies, and 312 in other countries. There were 11,000 Brothers, 1,000 in Paris.

novitiate for the region of Paris, but also many elderly and sick members of the order.

Brother Philippe, who had been superior general for sixteen years, died and was replaced by Brother Jean Olympe. But after only six months, he died suddenly and Brother Irlide took his place. Msgr. Debout reported that there were harmonious relations between the superiors of the house and their chaplain. The tasks of the chaplains were divided between Fr. Chaumont and Fr. Claude Antoine Tholon (1813–1896). The former preferred to celebrate daily Mass for the community at 6:00 a.m. and hear the confessions of the novices and aspirants and of the members of the minor novitiate. He took over, as well, the spiritual guidance of the Brothers who were aged or infirm. Fr. Tholon celebrated Sunday Mass, but the two priests took turns preaching the Sunday homily.

Msgr. Laveille, who gathered testimony from several of the Brothers, relates that Fr. Chaumont preached at Mass as much by his attitude of respect at the altar as by his conduct. This reverence for the Eucharist surely penetrated the Brothers in formation and was in turn transmitted to their future students.

The new chaplain felt the need to instruct more than to edify. He began a series of talks concerning the ceremonies of the Mass. Sometimes, while he explained the gestures of the priest at the altar, an exclamation of faith burst from his lips and touched the souls of his listeners. Speaking one day of the celebrant who gathers each crumb of consecrated bread after having communed, he exclaimed, "This is divine dust!" The tone of his voice was so vibrant that heads bowed in the church as they would for adoration.

His manner at the altar strengthened the faith of those attending. Here is the testimony of a survivor of those long-ago years: "He rapidly read the prayers up to the offertory. From that moment on he spoke slowly and seemed completely absorbed in awe at the act he was performing. He was so concentrated in his reverence for the sacrament he was carrying in the processions that he once admitted to a Brother never having noticed the magnificence of the monstrance." This priest, with his love of perfection, was at ease in the great silence of the house. The austere Rule of the disciples of St. Jean Baptiste de La Salle, their ceaseless work, their constant prayer in every moment not consecrated to carrying out their tasks, filled him with respect and sympathy. He spoke only with admiration of the Institute of Brothers and always had cordial relations with them.

The Work of St. Benedict Labre

Going beyond the responsibilities of a priest in this position, Fr. Chaumont participated with the Christian Brothers in the evangelization of youth in the suburbs, principally in organizing feasts of patron saints. With this purpose in mind, a new foundation was created. At the end of the yearly general assembly of youth ministries, Brother Exupérien proposed the formation of a group drawn from the best members and supported by the Brothers:

Among the assembly that has just dispersed, there must be some young people who could be formed into apostles by a spiritual culture stronger than that of the festivals of patron saints. We should find them, bring them together, give them special preparation, and use them to give more continuity to our projects.[254]

The two men rapidly brought together nine young people who founded the organization of St. Benedict Labre. The name was chosen to indicate how much they intended to differentiate themselves from worldly society.[255] Fr. Chaumont, who had too many commitments, confided the group to another priest who was under his spiritual guidance, Fr. Gabiller.[256] The organization developed rather well in the first years of the twentieth century:

---

[254]Quoted by Msgr. Laveille

[255]After several attempts at the religious life, Benedict Joseph Labre (1748-1783) took up the life of a pilgrim vagabond, a life of constant prayer. His reputation of saintliness spread rapidly attested to by reports of miracles. He was beatified in 1860, canonized in 1881. This organization of young people took his name right at this time.

Quoting Fr. Chaumont, Msgr. Debout said, "These young people have an admirable spirit of faith and of scorn for worldly society. They said to me, we want our patron to be Saint Labre, because he was covered with fleas. By that they meant that he despised the conventional social world and was despised by it. *(Summarium)*

[256]Charles Gabiller was a disciple of Msgr. de Ségur, who entered the Society of Priests of Saint Francis de Sales shortly after the death of the Blind Prelate. He died very young, at the age of 33, in 1886.

"St. Labre" brought several hundred priests and religious to the Church, thousands of devoted militants, the first participants in the nightly devotions at Montmartre, active participants in the lectures of St. Vincent de Paul, the employees union, the cradle of the CFTC (*Confédération française de travailleurs chrétiens*, Confederation of French Christian Workers), the founder of the JOC (*Jeunesse ouvrière catholique*, Young Catholic Workers) in France, and its first official priest. (R. Brion)

Fr. Chaumont decided to create an organization that would be associated with this one and that would support it with its prayers: "The Association of Prayers and Penitence for the Sanctification of Children and Youth of the Working Class."

"We appeal fervently to all people of faith and zeal to offer their prayers and works of penitence in order to obtain: 1) more priests and Christian school teachers to work for the education of children and youth; 2) that they will be so devoted to their work that their students will grow in faith; and 3) a renewed spirit in those who are already engaged in this profession, so that they recognize its saintly dimension." [257]

Act of Oblation

The retreat made during the summer of 1874 by Fr. Chaumont with the Redemptorists of Avon apparently marked a stage in his spiritual journey, encouraging him to offer himself even more. Hearing the members

---

[257] Quoted by Msgr. Laveille.

of the order flagellating each other, the priest was led to meditate more deeply on Jesus's scourging during his passion:

How is it possible to meditate a quarter of an hour on the flagellation of Jesus without feeling devoured by the desire to suffer with him? As we count the blows falling on him, how can we not cry out, "Enough! Now it is my turn." He was innocent; we are guilty, and we fear imposing some weak penance on ourselves to expiate our sins, when he suffered so much for us.[258]

Following this retreat, he pronounced the solemn offering of himself to God. Later he said that, although he had suffered a great deal in the following years, the fact that he had given this meaning to his pain brought him inner peace.

For many years, Fr. Chaumont kept secret the formula that he read at the time of his oblation, and revealed it only to his sister Marthe a few years before his death:

I, Henri Chaumont, poor and unworthy priest of Jesus Christ, considering that he who does not have the spirit of Jesus does not belong to Jesus, that wherever the spirit of Jesus reigns, the face of all things is renewed; considering that in our times, those who still call themselves Christians are more and more moved by worldly things, by a spirit that is the enemy of the spirit of God; considering that in times of such widespread evil, the appearance of devotion reduced to the observance of a few laws of the church and a

---

[258] Words reported by Mlle Anquier, a Daughter of St. Francis de Sales.

few good works is not enough to comfort the adorable heart of Jesus; considering that, not taking account of my unworthiness and my many sins and failings, it has pleased our Lord to use me to help bring back to life, among priests and their faithful, a spirit of docility toward his holy spirit; considering that, in order to cooperate with the works of Christ crucified, we must be united with him in love and in the spirit of sacrifice; deploring bitterly my past lack of courage and my unwillingness to check the protestations of nature, I accept with my whole spirit and all my strength, the pain, the trials, the crosses in every form and no matter how heavy that God may choose to send me. I offer all to him in union with the heart of Jesus, for the expiation of my own sins, so that by my humble efforts, joined with those of all the Church, the spirit of Jesus will penetrate abundantly into the hearts of priests and all Christians. Amen." [259]

At the same time he wrote the following lines, which emphasize once more his awareness of the value of offering his pain and sufferings for others:

I know nothing and I want to know nothing except this word that says it all: the Cross. It is the heaven of our earth.

The Cross . . . is the sign of salvation. Our Lord was marked by it; the souls who continue his work must also be. The Cross is the great book from which we learn of the goodness through which we have been

---

[259] Quoted by Msgr. Laveille.

redeemed and the misery in which we lived before this redemption.

Courage and confidence travel well together; if you are ready to renounce yourselves, carry your own cross every day, then follow Jesus to Calvary as you wait for him to lead you to paradise. Long live the cross! Everything that we suffer brings souls to salvation. What better reward could we hope for?" [260]

In this remark he professes a constant humility, which takes the form of thinking very little of his own qualities:

The feeling of his own powerlessness and unworthiness never left Fr. Chaumont. Some would be tempted to find his attitude exaggerated, especially when he claimed that it was time for him to disappear, to "melt away," as he said, and when he saw himself as an element of sterility and failure in his own undertakings. Until the end of his life he remained persuaded that the Society of Priests had come into being without his deserving any credit for it. "I walked with no idea of where I was headed. I did not set out with a clear idea of how to organize things. I had just enough vision to discern where I should put one foot ahead of the other, no more." (Notebook of Sister Ignace, quoted by Msgr. Debout.)

Father Chaumont's Position on Questions of Church Authority

---

[260] Quoted by Msgr. Debout.

Even though some of his fellow priests criticized his indulgence in the administration of the Sacrament of Penance, Fr. Chaumont was not at all a progressive. In his writings he emphasizes the duty of the clergy to respect papal authority. A good example is his response to the appearance of Pope Leo XIII's encyclical on free masonry (*Humanum genus*) April 20, 1884:

Rather than receiving this great and paternal act of the Sovereign Pontiff with veneration and gratitude, many of the baptized have dared to raise their voices against it, protesting that his stance is too severe. We see that the Christian spirit has not remained pure, even among the children of the Church. There is corruption by the spirit of the world, which is nothing other than the spirit of the devil. In the best families we can find people reading newspapers and reviews full of this spirit of rebellion. They are little by little fed this poison that undermines the true faith and the Christian life. This is why ordinary citizens who were good up until now begin to give in to bad influences." [261]

Fr. Chaumont judged the society of his time quite harshly, which he saw as aligned in opposition to the Church, a counter current to a society inspired by faith:

Worldly society is organized sin, not the non-believers whose conversion Jesus is seeking. . . . Worldly society is corrupt, even when, in appearance and outwardly,

---

[261] Talk given by Fr. Chaumont at the meeting of Priests, June 2, 1884, quoted by Msgr. Debout.

it pretends to do good. People have never spoken so much of equality, of good works and tolerance; we have never seen so many people self-righteously allied in welfare organizations, but under the surface the leaders are dedicated to tearing the masses away from the Church and putting an end to her. The measures that the Church has taken on behalf of the working people seem inspired by the desire to free them from all Christian influence. Worldly society tries in vain to teach lessons of wisdom and imagines that it can elevate minds by filling them with a stupid pride, improving their minds by moving them away from the temples of God. These good souls should give the common people the instruction and protection that others refuse them, and care for their poverty, which is a spiritual poverty. [262]

He also set himself apart from the debates that were the preludes to the modernist crisis. He snubbed Fr. Dufresne, a priest of St. Francis de Sales, who was close to what was then called "Americanism,"[263] and attacked vigorously the orientations of liberal Catholicism, which he saw as still present and active in the Church:

---

[262] Quoted by Msgr. Debout.

[263] This movement had several aspects. It seems that the debate in which Fr. François-Xavier Dufresne (1848–1900) participated, dealt with the priority that should be given to evangelization (the active virtues) over contemplation. A Jesuit, R. P. Watrigant, opposed him. In this affair Fr. Dufresne made it clear that his position was personal and did not represent the entire Society of Priests.

Liberalism means, "We must follow the times we live in and the evolution of ideas. The Pope has spoken; he has a right to do so; but what he is saying does not correspond to the tendencies and institutions of our times. Therefore, as long as it is not a question of dogma or an essential point of morals, we will continue to follow our own customs and feelings.

The profound liberalism of earlier times was first cousin to Protestantism. Liberal ideas today do not have such grave consequences but the principle is still the same. It is intellectual pride that translates into this formula: 'After all, we are free.' [264]

Liberal Catholics are essentially people led by reason. But our Lord said, "Father, I thank you that you have hidden these things from the wise and the powerful and revealed them to the lowly."

The liberal spirit is born of a complete lack of humility; it is anti-evangelical. I pray that God will protect my poor works! I would rather see them destroyed than infected by such a spirit of pride. [265]

Health Problems

Fr. Chaumont's numerous activities inevitably drained his strength. Nevertheless, he continued to devote a

---

[264] Fr. Chaumont returns here to a fundamental idea in Msgr. de Ségur's book *Revolution* (1860), which judges that the prideful revolt of humans against God (beginning with the original sin) is the basis of the evils of modern times.

[265] Notes of Miss Rousselet, quoted by Msgr. Laveille.

great deal of time to hearing confessions.[266] Additionally, he accompanied his colleague, Fr. Tholon, in his last illness. The young priest's death at the end of 1875 left him with even more responsibilities. He organized himself to take advantage of every instant:

He never wasted his time, said Miss Tonery [sic], who knew him. He practiced a "cult of minutes," even while eating his meals. He had invented a little desk so that he could read while at table and on Sundays he invited Mlle Anquier to his table so that he could take an English lesson. His mother reported that he had tried to read while he was shaving. He tried to always be perfectly on time. For the celebration of Mass, he was ready and waiting at the door of the sacristy and left at the first strike of the hour. As soon as Mass was completed he went directly to his confessional, left at 8:00 to eat a breakfast that lasted only a few minutes; the rest of the day was measured out in a similar way. In the evening, in the solitude of his quarters, he continued to work. (Msgr. Debout)

All of this brought on a new crisis of rheumatism beginning on May 9, 1876, which immobilized him for two months and became so severe that his followers feared for his life. His Daughters prayed constantly for their reverend father. Nevertheless, he spent a little time with his family:

---

[266] "At one Christmas Eve Mass he was seen losing his balance at the altar as he celebrated and it became known that he had been hearing confessions since 6:00 a.m. with only brief pauses for his meals." (Msgr. Laveille)

Fr. Chaumont's profoundly cheerful nature was never eclipsed. As his mother aged,[267] he felt that greater affection that brings us closer to lives that are drawing to a close; and he showed that affection on each important anniversary through compliments or poems that always had a little note of tenderness or wit, bringing tears with her smiles. His sister's gentle devotion was one of the dearest fruits of his brotherly attention. But it was especially in the company of his brother Ernest that he experienced the deepest emotions, even joy, that remained with him for many days. Ernest Chaumont was vice president of the Circle of Montparnasse, a member of the lecturers of St. Vincent de Paul, father of a model family, an outstanding Christian, simple and straightforward, capable of the greatest devotion to others. His talents as a musician earned him the position of organist at Saint Nicholas du Chardonnet, and then at the Collège de Juilly. His brother Henri felt kinship with his joyful and sincere nature and they were very close.

The two brothers exchanged witty remarks and subtle jokes, even light-hearted rhymes, since they both had a talent for verse. These were moments of innocent happiness for the priest who was so often burdened with worries. (Msgr. Laveille)

Given his health problems, due at least in part to exhaustion brought on by his many duties, he found himself one day torn between the advice of both Fr.

---

[267] She was living with him at that time, 10 rue Monsieur.

Landon[268] and Fr. Tissot,[269] the first suggesting that he should rest, the latter seeing in his abundance of responsibilities the sign of his faithful service to our Lord.

We have only spoken of my present situation, internal and external. Truth obliges me to say that at the enumeration of all that I am suffering, Fr. Tissot, whose great heart I know so well, began to laugh and to clap his hands. "Bravo! Bravo!" he said. "How happy I am to know that you are in such a state! Ah! You think that you will have such an abundance of chances to serve our Lord and that it won't cost you anything? That you won't be humiliated? That you won't be exhausted physically and emotionally? Good work; it is all necessary in the name of God's justice."

I tried to attempt this protest . . . "But I am suffering so much in my spirit from the pain in my body, that I would like to be cured of this inner martyrdom."

"Be careful not to ask for that," replied the priest. "You need it." And he added, "As for being exhausted, what difference does that make? Priests pampering

---

[268] After the death of Msgr. de Ségur, Fr. Emile Landon (1843–1911) was Fr. Chaumont's choice for spiritual director. In 1903 Fr. Landon was chosen as director for the Daughters of St. Francis de Sales.

[269] After Fr. Landon asked to be relieved of the task of spiritual director of Fr. Chaumont, he turned to Fr. Tissot, the superior of the missionaries of Saint-Francis de Sales, who was introduced to him by Fr. Emmanuel de la Perche. Fr. Tissot died in 1894. Fr. Chaumont then asked a Jesuit living in Paris, Fr. Pitot, to accompany him through the last years of his life.

themselves? My God! Unforgivable. Priests should die from their overwork. You, rest? More likely you would be engaged in pleasant chatter with doctors in a society salon. Get on with it! However exhausted and broken you may feel, look for more work. Is good being done? Yes. Well, then, why would you want to be cured?" [270]

Preaching Retreats for Priests

Another task was added to Fr. Chaumont's responsibilities. It happened in a perfectly logical way: Fr. Tissot asked him to join in the ministry of preaching retreats to priests. Fr. Chaumont hesitated for a long time. It required all the persuasive powers of Mme Carré to make him accept.[271] He began this ministry at the end of July 1886, addressing the faculty of the Paris minor seminary, meeting at the Maison d'Athis. A few weeks later he spoke to the students of the major seminary at Vannes, called by the superior, Fr. Lair, who knew of him through his writings on spiritual direction. Fr. Chaumont asked the Daughters and the Priests of St. Francis de Sales to pray for him when he undertook this new mission.

In January 1887, he continued this undertaking at the major seminary of Périgueux. Then he went, in that

---

[270] Msgr. Debout July 13, 1883, quotes Fr. Chaumont's letter to Fr. Landon.

[271] "She became 'nearly indiscreet.' I don't know what evil spirit was tormenting me, but I couldn't make up my mind. I just didn't dare. The Reverend Mother was too much for me." Declaration of Fr. Chaumont at the retreat for the Daughters of St. Francis de Sales in 1895, quoted by Msgr. Debout.

same year, to Dijon, Dôle, Lyon, and Fribourg, where he was reunited with Fr. Merillod, and on to Orléans, Paray-le-Monial, Aurillac, and Condé-sur-Noireau. Invited by Msgr. Lelong to preach a retreat for the diocesan priests of Nevers, he asked to be excused, on the grounds that he was too tired. Indeed, he had been obliged to rest for a short time at Athis with the Brothers, then at Sainte-Adresse. But Fr. Tissot insisted that he continue preaching. This meant fifteen days of uninterrupted work (the first half of September 1888) because it was necessary to divide the priests making the retreat into two successive groups. At the end of this exhausting exercise, which had allowed Fr. Chaumont to further develop his ideas about the importance of spiritual direction, Msgr. Lelong named him honorable Canon of his Cathedral. The following year, in July, he led the retreat for priests at Luçon, then the retreat d'Athis for the Priests of St. Francis de Sales. There followed two retreats at Auch.

The *Religious Weekly* of the diocese reported:

Fr. Chaumont does not deliver solemn sermons, which are hardly appropriate for pastoral retreats. He gives lectures, conversations, genres in which he is a master. The informal tone that he adopts takes nothing away from the nobility of his language and the lofty content of his thought. He is an artist in the development of his subject matter. He has a talent for diction; he is charming, warm, distinguished, deeply spiritual, and thoroughly familiar with the situation of priests. His audience was delighted and instructed.

Fr. Chaumont distinguishes himself by his knowledge of the spiritual life, almost as much as by his talent as an orator. Many of the priests who heard him bought his principle book, Monseigneur de Ségur, finding in it a faithful echo of the teachings of the retreat, taken from the book and the heart of that gentle and saintly prelate.[272]

In 1890 he gave another retreat for the Priests of St. Francis de Sales at La Salette; in the summer of 1891, in response to a request from Cardinal Place, he preached also for the priests in Rennes. The Cardinal then asked for documentation concerning the Society of Priests of St. Francis de Sales for himself. requesting as well that it be forwarded to the superior of the major seminary so that he also could spread Fr. Chaumont's ideas. When the priest left Rennes, he visited the Salesian groups at Moulins and Périgueux before going to Lourdes to participate in the retreat of the Society preached by Fr. Joseph Paguelle de Follenay (1852–1899).[273] But he had to hurry on to another retreat at Rodez, returning to Paris via Aurillac and Nevers.

The next year he preached the retreat for about 100 members of the Society of Priests at Athis, and at the end of summer 1893, he addressed the priests of the diocese of Troyes, answering the request of Bishop Msgr. Cortet.

---

[272] *Religious Weekly of Auch,* October 19, 1889, quoted by Msgr. Laveille

[273] He succeeded Fr. Chaumont at the motherhouse of the Brothers in July 1889. He wrote a biography of Cardinal Guibert and became vice-rector of the Catholic Institute of Paris in 1892.

Speaking with a new group of his fellow priests, Fr. Chaumont limited himself to discussing the notion of the priesthood in simple but comprehensive terms. Basing his talk on the words of St. Paul, "homo Dei," he described all of the spiritual and human obligations of their vocation. But in speaking with those who came to him for spiritual guidance he was always careful to temper his instruction and counsel with unlimited mercy and gentleness. (Msgr. Laveille)

He continued his tour with a retreat at the monastery of the Visitation in Poligny, then a retreat for priests in Dijon in September 1893 and finally in Poitiers, where he was welcomed by his former classmate in the seminary of Montmorillon, Fr. Bougouin, superior of the major seminary.

Sometimes he did not preach himself. He just attended the retreats of the Society. It was not really less work for him because the participants all wanted some time with him. Fr. Chaumont began a journey with Fr. Lenfant to visit the groups of priests of the Society as he had done in 1893–1894. He first returned to Brussels, then to Aix-la-Chapelle. From there he continued to Rouen and Le Havre, before taking the train to Marseilles to bid farewell to the new Missionary Catechists. He returned to Paris by way of Nice, Privas, and Lyon. In the summer of 1894, there was another tour of retreats in which he was joined by Fr. Debout, traveling to the major seminaries of Poitier, Angoulême, Cognac, and finally to Lourdes for the retreat of the Priests of St. Francis de Sales from the dioceses of the Midi, preached by Fr. Dufresne.[274] On his return to Paris he made several more stops to visit groups of priests of the Society at Périgueux, Aurillac, Le Puy, Clermont, Moulins, and Nevers.

The retreat of the Priests of St. Francis de Sales, which began July 29,1895, at Athis, was the last one for Fr. Chaumont. He was exhausted. Fr. Lenfant preached the retreat but the founder spoke once a day.

It was very difficult for him to attend. He traveled by carriage, because he was unable to withstand the journey by train. In spite of his extreme fatigue he was present for the instructions and spoke at the end of the two-hour lecture, exhorting the members to uphold the traditions of the dear family, the spirit of Salesian love, the supernatural spirit, and the spirit of evangelization. He repeated these words: "Tenete traditions" (maintain your traditions). This persistence had a ring of sadness, like a farewell, more so since he had said shortly before that ten more years would be necessary for the Society to be all that it should be.

The closing took place Friday, August 2, in the morning. Our reverend Father had intended for some time to present a gift of gratitude to the dear Christian Brothers who had provided us such warm and generous hospitality every three years. He bought a beautiful statue of St. Francis de Sales that was placed in a monumental niche in one of the most beautiful

---

[274] A word spoken by Fr. Dufresne led Fr. Chaumont to realize that it was his last visit to Lourdes.

wooded areas of the park. After the formal closing during which three of our brother priests made their profession, we went in procession to the feet of the statue. Our dear Father blessed it after expressing for all of us the thankfulness that filled our hearts. There is no need to add that great joy mixed with the sadness of having to leave one another too soon penetrated our last meal together.[275]

Jubilee of the Founder

The twenty-fifth anniversary of the ordination of Fr. Chaumont occurred in 1889. Because of serious health problems he decided to leave his position with the Brothers. Brother Irlilde asked that he be given a distinction to recognize his years of service. Cardinal Richard offered him the position of titular canon but Fr. Chaumont refused, fearing that his failing health would keep him from daily attendance at Mass. He became instead an honorary canon of Paris.

The Daughters, who now numbered 736, offered him a beautiful priestly vestment. The Priests of the Society presented him with a beautiful chalice and two albums in which all the members of the two spiritual families had inscribed their words of gratitude.

The Last Years
In 1891 Fr. Chaumont moved to an apartment at 82 rue de Varenne, in order to be closer to the Daughters who then were living on the rue de Bourgogne. His mother

---

[275] *Bulletin of the Society of Priests of Saint Francis de Sales,* August 1895.

went to live with him. Mlle Toneri, one of the Daughters, spoke about Mme Chaumont:

Mme Chaumont was beautifully devout, the true image of the "strong woman" of the Gospels. Her house was always perfectly in order and run with frugality. She confessed frequently to her son and received Communion every day. . . . I had the honor and the pleasure to be invited to a meal with her. I have always admired the veneration and respect of the mother for the son and vice-versa. (Summarium)

At this time Fr. Chaumont wrote a brochure, "The Method of Saint Francis de Sales in Spiritual Direction," with the purpose of demonstrating how closely the saint's thinking followed the Gospel itself. He wrote:

Everything that we admire in the saintly doctor, his gentleness, goodness, and patience, his fervor in working for the salvation of souls, everything that his experience in this ministry inspired in him in order to win souls for Christ, all of this springs from his remaining faithful in every point to the methods of the Gospel.

A group of Priests of St. Francis de Sales began to gather in 1894 to assist with his many responsibilities. He found a residence nearly facing the "House of the Good God" on the rue de Bourgogne:

First came Fr. Bornel, who was already working with his ministry, although he was responsible for another institution in Paris; Msgr. Faralicq, salaried canon of

Belley, who gave up his seat in the Chapter to devote himself to the Society of Priests of St. Francis de Sales; and Fr. Debout, who had learned to respect and admire Fr. Chaumont in the course of their travels together, and who gave up a position as director of the Collège of Arras in order to be with the founder. A little later two other men joined the group, Fr. Monnier, canon of Saint Claude[276] and Canon Costaz, administrator of the Catholic Institute of Paris. (Msgr. Laveille)

It was principally from this group that Fr. Chaumont chose those who would help with his projects. Msgr. Debout described the atmosphere around the table with the founder and his mother:

The meals were always served exactly on time, beginning and ending with a prayer recited with fervent devotion by Fr. Chaumont, prayers to which his mother responded from the depth of her own faith. The food was simple but satisfying; the conversation always pleasant, from time to time sparkling with the special wit of Parisians, but never becoming coarse. Fr. Chaumont never forgot that he was a priest; he remained constantly in contact with God. Completely at the disposition of his guests, his gaze always turned to his dearly beloved Jesus. He was at all times respectful of his mother and she treated her priest-son with respectful tenderness.

---

[276] Fr. Laurent Monnier (1847–1927) became bishop of Troyes in 1907.

The members of the household always referred to Mme Chaumont as 'Dear Mother.' Filled with the supernatural strength that her son accorded to his spiritual children, she also adopted them in God's eyes and gave them all of the tenderness of a grandmother. That's why we named her as we did.

Nevertheless. reorganization became necessary. The priests wanted Fr. Chaumont to live with them,[277] while his mother would move in with the Daughters in the "House of the Good God." Another move, this time to 8 avenue de Tourville.[278] In 1894 there were six priests accompanying Fr. Chaumont: Frs. Bornel, Costaz, Debout, Dufresne, Faralicq, and Monnier.

At five minutes before noon, we had a meeting in the chapel, where we performed our "particular examens" in silence.[279] Then we went to the dining room, where, after the blessing and thanksgiving, we listened to some verses from the Gospels or from "The Imitation of Christ". During the meal, the conversation, led by Fr. Chaumont, was instructive and interesting. It centred on the events of the day, especially things that concerned the Society, because there were always a number of tasks under way to be discussed. We were sometimes light-hearted, as was

---

[277] Msgr. said, "Our community was missing its head."

[278] After the death of Fr. Chaumont, the little "fatherless" community remained in the house at 8 avenue de Tourville until the lease was up, then they moved again to 22 rue de Varenne. In 1924 Fr. Debout acquired the building at number 22 to give a fixed center to the Society.

[279] This was a rapid review of one's conscience, a review before God of the morning's happenings.

Father, but he never let a remark that could be interpreted as off-color go by without a reprimand. He wanted limits in humor as in everything.

Nevertheless, life with the priest was joyful. The meetings alternating between the two Paris groups were lively, because at that time the meetings scheduled to begin at 5:45 in the afternoon were followed by a meal in common. And even outside these regularly scheduled events, whenever an occasion presented itself, Fr. Chaumont, unless there was a feast day or he was exceptionally tired, asked that there should be something extra. Often his health kept him from participating himself. In the evening we were together in the chapel at five minutes before seven. After dinner we met in the living room. Our period of relaxation continued for a half hour. We sometimes played chess or checkers or trictrac, (a board game similar to backgammon), but most often we chatted.

After recreation time, one of us read out loud from a book chosen by the founder, and once a week the "mea culpa" (recognition of one's faults). Fr. Chaumont would have liked this exercise to be more frequent but we decided on once a week. An evening prayer in the chapel ended the day. (Msgr. Debout)

Mme Chaumont passed away very shortly thereafter, on January 14, 1895. Her death was very difficult for her son and the more so because his own health was failing. His heart trouble and his rheumatism kept him from undertaking any more major travel, a responsibility he entrusted to Fr. Monnier.

Fr. Chaumont himself, while continuing his administrative duties, returned to his work of evangelization in his living area. Conversions of even the most obstinate sinners, abjuration of heretics, adult baptism, revalidation of marriages, confessions of religious sisters, preaching of all kinds, study groups concerning spiritual direction for the Priests or Sons of Saint Francis de Sales, plus a very active correspondence, filled his days and part of his nights.
(Msgr. Laveille)

He lived his last years in constant preparation for death:

I understand that a good religious sister may slip away peacefully, that she may not especially worry about her salvation. But I don't understand how I, who have had the responsibility of founding a Society, have decided so many questions and made so many decisions, how could I not be concerned about the judgments of God? My responsibilities have been greater than those of a simple Christian. I am not anxious because I count on God's mercy. Still and all, I have been living for a long time face to face with this thought: God's judgment. I can say that I take no action without considering the judgment of our Good Lord. [280]

However, such thoughts did not trouble his deep inner peace:

---

[280] Manuscript memoirs of Mother Mary of Jesus (Mlle Stiltz) quoted by Msgr. Laveille.

Last January when I thought I was going to die, and it might have been the end, because I could hardly breathe—I said to myself while they went to bring a priest, "Will he get here in time?" But I was not for a minute afraid. I said to myself, "After all, the good Lord knows that I love him." I tried to recite acts of perfect love and I remained calm.[281]

This inner peace was not the manifestation of a spiritual life marked by extraordinary graces:

As he expressed it himself, the altar and the tabernacle were made of bronze. He had to perform the divine act in the silence of God. But this state of mind, in appearance so rigorous, speeded his process of detachment and his progress toward the purest love. (Msgr. Laveille)

He wrote to Mme Carré:

Pray a great deal for me. Every day I have more need of prayers. I withstand my forced labor, condemned in perpetuity, without strength; I love my ball and chain through my spirit of reparation and my love of divine justice, but my lack of courage calls out from time to time for a word from on high. Nevertheless, those voices are still, and abandon me to myself, that is to my own poverty of spirit and suffering in all its possible forms. Pray for me. I find myself abject.[282]

---

[281] Manuscript memoirs of Mlle Anquier, quoted by Msgr. Laveille.

[282] Letter of Fr. Chaumont to Mme Carré, September 19, 1889, quoted by Msgr. Debout.

Msgr. Laveille wrote about his attraction for certain devotions:

From the beginning, Fr. Chaumont had recommended to the Daughters first of all devotion to the Holy Spirit, principal of all supernatural love, but he wanted to give his personal example. Every time that the liturgy permitted it, he celebrated a votive mass of the Holy Spirit in a chapel lighted and decorated as if for a feast day.[283]

His devotion to the Holy Eucharist led him to reserve the finest and most precious vessels for the sacrament. Following the beliefs of Msgr. de Ségur, he was one of the first and most fervent advocates of daily Communion.

His love for the Holy Eucharist was most evident by his attitude at the altar. . . . Seeing him in so much pain, his colleagues wanted to spare him the fatigue of celebrating Mass. But he insisted, saying, "You don't know what passes between Jesus and the priest at the altar."

This tender devotion to God-made-man led logically to his devotion to the Sacred Heart. From the beginning Fr. Chaumont wanted the feast of the Sacred Heart to be one of the patronal feasts of the Daughters, and he had it celebrated with all solemnity. . . . In 1880 he composed and distributed a prayer that

---

[283] All of the chapels of the Society are dedicated to the Holy Spirit.

expressed exactly the spirituality he wanted to bring to the forefront.

Full of respect for the Word of God contained in the Scriptures, he had made it a rule for his Daughters to read the New Testament every year and to kiss its pages every evening.

His filial devotion to the Blessed Virgin took the form of many practices in honor of the Immaculate Conception, by his choice of "Mary Immaculate" as patron of his wonderful association of prayers, and also by the solemn procession held on December 8th at the "House of the Good God." The image of Our Lady of Perpetual Help that he had had placed in the chapels of all Salesian groups testified as well to the strength of his devotion to Mary. The guardian angels had to be invoked at least five times a day in the daily prayers of the Daughters; St. Joseph was protector and steward of the "House of the Good God." (Msgr. Laveille)

At the end of the summer of 1895 Fr. Chaumont's health took a serious turn for the worse. After several days' rest at le Mans, he again became weaker and had to return to Paris. There he seemed to improve and was able to go back to work writing a brochure on the methods of spiritual direction of St. Francis de Sales, his testimony for the process of beatification of Mme Carré, and other concerns for the Societies. His enlarged heart worsened in the spring of 1896, causing severe difficulty breathing and interfering with his sleep.

For many weeks he struggled against the illness. It got to the point that he could only celebrate Mass supported by two fellow priests. But the day came when even this joy became impossible for him and he had to accept that he could only attend one of the Masses in the House. A carriage always driven by the same coachman arrived every morning in the little courtyard of the avenue de Tourville and stopped in front of the house as close as possible to the door. With the help of a priest, the sick man got into the carriage, which drove slowly to the "House of the Good God." There Fr. Chaumont went to his office next to the chapel, opened a door that separated him from the chapel, and set to work in sight of the tabernacle. He spent his day either in the confessional or in administrative duties, and in the evening, driven by the same coachman, he returned to the avenue Tourville to preside over the meal with his brother priests. (Msgr. Laveille)

His condition worsened again at the time of the retreat for the Daughters preached by Fr. Dufresne at the "House of the Good God." He attended a last Council of the Society, but when he returned to his residence he took to his bed, never able to get up again. He died May 15, 1896, at 10:30 in the evening at the age of fifty-eight.

More than two hundred priests of the Society of Priests of St. Francis de Sales were present at Notre Dame for his funeral, celebrated by the dean of the Cathedral

Chapter in the presence of three Vicars General of Paris and Msgr. d'Hulst.[284]

His Writing and Homilies

Msgr. Debout emphasized the breadth of the oratorical works of Fr. Chaumont:

We know that he spoke easily and often in public: at Sainte Clotilde, every time that he presided at evening prayer; there are instructions on the mysteries of the Rosary for every day of the month of May; then there are talks given during Lent; daily talks generally on the subject of the Gospel of the day; more than fifteen sermons dealing with the month of St. Joseph; a series of seventeen conversations on the subject of temptation; another series on the witnesses present at the Passion; and on the instruments of torture used on Our Lord.
Briefly, in the papers that have been preserved, there are elements of more than six hundred talks.

It is fitting to add to the texts written by Fr. Chaumont the notes that were taken by his listeners, especially those taken by the Daughters of St. Francis de Sales. He spoke to them at least a thousand times. There are several different sermons on the same passage of the Gospel. There are traces of about fifteen retreats, even though he preached many more. Often there is only an outline or a simple draft. Once the outline was finished, Father worked out many subdivisions,

---

[284] Cardinal Richard had come the first evening to pay his respects to the deceased.

sometimes as many as six, showing that the topic was indeed treated in depth. It is possible that for certain outlines he followed the models of Msgr. de Ségur.

During the process of beatification led by the Ordinary (1923–1930), fifty-five witnesses were heard: fifteen priests of the Society; five others, among them Paul Chaumont, Fr. Chaumont's nephew; and twenty-eight Daughters, twenty-five single and three married women. Three of the Daughters were missionaries in non-Christian countries, one in a Christian area. There was also a Benedictine religious sister (a former Daughter of St. Francis de Sales), a Jesuit and a Redemptorist. The five laypersons quoted had family connections: a niece of Msgr. de Ségur and four relatives of Fr. Chaumont, his sister Madeleine, and a nephew by marriage, Joseph Bottard, and his wife Marie-Louise. Mlle Tessier gave one of the most insightful analyses of the faith and life of the priest:

He lived his faith and he knew how to communicate it to others. He was filled with the sense of his responsibility, and the idea of God's judgment was always in his mind. Therefore, he tried to do his best to act according to God's will. His faith was as profound as it was simple, guiding him to follow and understand God's ways in spiritual guidance. His faith was straightforward and strong; it inspired and directed all of his devotions, most importantly devotion to the Holy Spirit, to the Blessed Sacrament, and to the Holy Virgin.

His devotion to Jesus in the Blessed Sacrament was profound, and already as a young priest he could not bear to think of the Lord present in the Eucharist, left alone through entire nights. He advised those under his spiritual guidance to go into the churches they passed to greet Jesus present in the Host. He suggested that when one visited the sacrament, it was preferable to converse with the Lord concerning his interests, thinking of what would bring him greater glory, rather than to speak to him always about ourselves. (Summarium)

Discipline and measure were always the rule of his life. He abhorred the superfluous that could lead to giving free rein to our natural instincts, and interfere with the workings of grace. To the practice of measure and discipline he always voluntarily added mortification and penance, as much to keep his own instincts in check as to expiate the sins of the recalcitrant and merit the graces of conversion, salvation, and sanctification for all souls. In his own discipline, Fr. Chaumont knew how to remain reasonable; for those in his spiritual care, he watched carefully that no excesses in that area would harm their health or interfere with their functions in life. (Summarium)

Fr. Chaumont possessed a great spiritual austerity; he felt no special gentleness toward himself but he had great tenderness (unction[285]) for others. In him there was special communication with the Holy Spirit that

---

[285] This word, rarely used in contemporary religious life, was frequent in the nineteenth century, especially in describing the manner of speaking of certain priests. It evoked a gentle intonation intended to touch the listeners.

he radiated when he spoke about God, and he worked always to develop this gentleness in his Daughters; at the same time he wanted them to be strong and courageous.[286]

---

[286] The last sentence well indicates the desire that Fr. Chaumont had for his Daughters: that they would develop a combination of strength of soul and gentleness in its expression.

CONCLUSION

The life of Fr. Henri Chaumont is an accurate reflection of the religious life of France in the nineteenth century and more particularly, that of the diocese of Paris in the second half of that century. There were indeed many priests but also many tasks for them to perform. The attendance at Mass in a parish such as Sainte Clotilde could give a false impression of the larger state of the faith in Paris, leading many priests to limit themselves to their strictly priestly duties. But Fr. Chaumont saw with greater lucidity that many areas of the city were barely formed in the life of the Church. He saw that situation as soon as he took his first assignment as assistant in the new and densely populated parish of Saint Marcel. This situation reminded him of his concern for the evangelization of areas that had never been reached by Christianity, a concern that had begun in his early childhood with the reading of *Annals of the Propagation of the Faith.*

In his priestly ministry he began by using the classic methods practiced by the Church since the Council of Trent: celebration of the Eucharist, preaching, catechism, confessions, and spiritual direction. Of course, he recognized the need for adaptations. When speaking to the workers of Saint Marcel he was careful to make his language simple and appealing, adding song and instrumental music. He took his inspiration from organizations such as the Society of St. Francis Xavier, asking laypeople, in this case his father, to give talks on non-religious subjects in order to overcome some of the anticlericalism present in these social groups. His concern for his parishioners led him to face the dangers of difficult areas of the city in order to take the sacraments to them.

When he was named assistant of Sainte Clotilde, he found himself in a situation that was the opposite of Saint Marcel. He was now among the most elegant society of Paris. Fortunately, the confidence of Msgr. de Ségur had prepared him for the spiritual direction of some of the women of this milieu. This task very quickly became the most important of his ministry and oriented his responsibilities in a decisive way.

He had discovered the spirituality of St. Francis de Sales while he was in the seminary. Msgr. de Ségur encouraged him to further this study and it became a precious aid in his ministry. Some of the women whom he met in the confessional at Sainte Clotilde wanted to lead a true life of faith, but the social rank of their husbands imposed certain restrictions on them. Following in the paths traced by *Introduction to the Devout Life,* he wanted to help them to overcome the supposed incompatibility between these two poles, though he refused all compromise with the "spirit of worldly society," even with social customs that most considered innocent (shaking a woman's hand, for instance). This led to his reputation of severity as a confessor, though he was always available for women who were able to overcome their fears and begin a journey of conversion. His pastoral methods following the beliefs of St. Francis de Sales led him to guide those under his spiritual direction with gentleness, helping them to set goals for themselves that they could reach, and thereby move forward steadily. He did not think in terms of a confession limited to rote enumeration of sins in fulfilment of a Church obligation. He thought in terms of true spiritual direction, seeking to understand the natural tendencies of each person he led, believing that grace does not work against our nature but seeks to perfect it.

His intention was first to lead the faithful to give up their own will—first by tearing down the old imperfect structures, then building anew, giving yourself over to God's will. Even if that goal was ambitious, Fr. Chaumont insisted that we must keep it always in our sights. He emphasized that, led with gentleness and compassion, the goal can be met.

From a human point of view he knew that the great problem of the nineteenth century was "social respect," which kept men especially away from the sacraments for fear of how people would speak of their conduct. For this reason, as soon as a man converted, Fr. Chaumont required that he be open about his commitment in order to encourage others to overcome their hesitations about becoming practicing Catholics.

In the writings of St. Francis de Sales, Fr. Chaumont saw the close connection between love of God and love of neighbor, a theme that seemed to be lacking in the spiritual "nothingness" (*néantisime)* of the French school of spirituality that was followed by the Sulpician professors at the seminary. Their goal appeared to be first of all personal perfection.

Meeting Mme Carré opened for him the possibility of an apostolate formed by the women of the upper classes in Paris. The Society of Christian Women disappointed him because many of the members lacked perseverance at a time when the conflict sharpened between the values of the Church and those of a society becoming ever more secular. The Daughters of St. Francis de Sales, to whom he then entrusted this responsibility, kept their promises with the spiritual guidance of Mme Carré and later Mlle Stiltz. Following the precepts of the saintly bishop of Geneva, Fr. Chaumont invited them to develop both their gentleness and their courage.

This interpenetration of evangelization and spirituality avoided two difficulties: the superficiality that made religion into a simple ornament of life in the spirit of the world with no true influence on daily living, and an activism that could push out all attempts at spiritual growth in the quest for the Kingdom of God. Here the figure of St. Francis de Sales makes its appearance, the first religious thinker to show how to live the life of evangelization and yet remain fully in the world of secular society.

At first the novelty of the way of life adopted by the Daughters made it difficult even for them to clearly define their situation. They were laywomen who sought to unite spirituality and evangelization beyond the usual limits of a church-related association, but they were not a community of religious sisters (they took no vows and many of them were married and mothers). The first Daughters felt this ambiguity, and used (among themselves) a vocabulary like that of a religious congregation.

Within the group it was difficult, at least at first, to articulate the relative authority of the founder and the general directress. This ambiguity was increased when Mme Carré moved away from Paris and again when she became ill. Nevertheless, as all gained more experience and Fr. Chaumont placed greater confidence in Mme Carré, the situation seemed to stabilize. Eventually the Society took a form resembling *Action Catholique,* at least for those who were most committed. Fr. Chaumont had to be very tactful in his presentation of the Society to the Archbishop who was concerned about maintaining his authority over this new form of Catholic organization. Msgr. d'Hulst was instrumental in allowing the group to exist officially in Paris, until Pope Pius X recognized it in 1911.

It was Vatican II that finally gave full recognition to the value of a ministry of evangelization led by lay Christians by virtue of their Baptism. In Fr. Chaumont's time, it was much more difficult to understand the place of such an apostolate in relationship to the clergy, who seemed to be the only legitimate channel between the faithful and the Lord.

In his letter to Msgr. Lelong, the bishop of Nevers, Fr. Chaumont explained that the Daughters were in no way in competition with the clergy but were a new form of collaboration, allowing the priestly ministry to be more effective and fruitful. Far from taking something away from the priest's role in spiritual direction the *Probatrices* among the Daughters were to be seen as experienced friends, whose duties were concerned only with the observation of the Rule and did not touch the areas reserved for the confessional.

The apostolate of women founded by Fr. Chaumont was not restricted to the more privileged classes. He turned as well to groups of women who were often marginalized in classical pastoral care, primary school teachers and housekeepers for priests, for example. In this he followed the model of Msgr. de Ségur, who worked closely with soldiers and the working class. His lifelong concern for missionary work led Fr. Chaumont to respond to appeals from bishops working overseas by creating the Catechist Missionaries, who worked with the clergy to bring the Gospel to un-Christianized peoples.[287]

Fr. Chaumont, who had worked with the population in the area of Saint Marcel, was also among the first to recognize the lack of a solid Christian formation in Paris itself. As chaplain for the Christian Brothers, he often accompanied the priests as they organized feasts of patron saints in different parishes and helped with the creation of the Society of St. Benedict Laboré. Supporting this mission, several Catechist Missionaries joined in service to the "difficult" areas of Paris.

---

[287] As proof of their sense of an evangelizing mission, the first Catechists who arrived in Nagpur were not content to limit themselves to opening dispensaries and doing charitable works, as the clergy wished, but wanted to go to the people as bearers of the Gospel.

Henri Chaumont had always had the greatest respect for the priesthood.[288] After the foundation of the Daughters of St. Francis de Sales, he had the idea of founding a Society of Priests who would share the spirituality of the Daughters. These priests would give an important part of their ministry to spiritual direction of the Daughters, with the purpose of forming a Christian elite. Fr. Chaumont, who was careful that the bishops would not take umbrage when encountering these societies, encouraged cooperation among the priests, even going so far as to suggest that they live in community, something that was not the rule in the nineteenth century.[289] Judging correctly that spiritual direction could be a means for striving toward perfection for priests themselves, Fr. Chaumont seems to be foreshadowing the language of Vatican II, which invites priests to seek their own perfection through the practice of their ministry.

In exercising the ministry of spirit and justice (cf. 2 Cor 9) the Priests of St. Francis de Sales take root in the spiritual life, provided that they welcome the spirit of Christ, which gives them life and guides them. It is their liturgical acts of every day that direct their lives toward perfection; it is their whole ministry, carried out in communion with the bishops and other priests. .

---

[288] See, for example, the letter he wrote to his parents at the time of his ordination, end of Chapter I.

[289] The rigid hierarchy of the clergy, which was in part a result of the *Concordat,* led to isolation, even in living conditions, at least in the big cities. During his period as vicar at Sainte Clotilde, Fr. Chaumont was obliged to rent an apartment for himself. Several bishops, for example, Msgr. Dupanloup, tried with a modicum of success to force priests to live a "life in common."

. . It is the loyal, tireless exercise of their work in the spirit of Christ that constitutes for priests the authentic means to arrive at holiness.[290]

For them, as for the Daughters, spiritual life and evangelization should be intertwined.

In the retreats that he preached to priests, though he made an effort not to impose himself by an authoritative attitude,[291] Fr. Chaumont's approach was demanding: he directed his listeners to a path of humility, simplicity, and generosity. He called on them to maintain a dignified demeanor, to present an attitude of warmth and friendliness, to be always courteous and welcoming, to give tirelessly in their ministry. In the Sacrament of Penance he advocated rigor in demands and gentleness in attitude.

Inner discipline should be strict, as he saw it, but the approach should be encouraging. He wanted religion to be attractive. This is Salesian gentleness, the only way to win hearts to Jesus, as Msgr. Mollevant taught Gaston de Ségur, who in turn transmitted it to his disciple. Fr. Chaumont experienced this at first with his ministry at Saint Marcel among the poor, and felt it all the more as he visited the wounded in Paris hospitals during the war of 1870. He continued in the same spirit when he began his work as assistant at Sainte Clotilde with parishioners who were

---

[290] See Vatican Council II decree, *Presbytorum ordinis,* on the Ministry and the Life of Priests, nos. 12–13.

[291] As mentioned, he refused the title of "superior general" although he had that role and was recognized as exercising those functions.

completely different, the women of the upper classes of Paris society for whom he became confessor. But his true goal was spiritual direction.[292] In his efforts to lead those he guided away from the values of "worldly society," which contradict the doctrines of the Gospel, he did not hesitate to harshly criticize the surrounding society and to condemn Catholic liberalism, which he saw as a compromise with the perverted values of his time.[293] Nevertheless, this severity in language had to be adapted to the strengths of those he counseled and practiced with gentleness and generosity.[294]

Following the example of the saintly bishop of Geneva, he alternated demands and encouragements in spiritual guidance. Salesian spirituality, far from denying the reality of sin and the influence of sin, brings a human quality that softens the "nothingness" (*néantisme*) of the French school. As a spiritual

---

[292] Even though one of the societies founded by Fr. Chaumont sought to engage laymen, the Sons of Francis de Sales, his pastoral work was essentially with women, a sign of the "feminization" of religion in the nineteenth century. Here Fr. Chaumont's work differed from that of Msgr. de Ségur, but they dedicated an equal amount of time to confessions.

[293] Impossible to be more severe in the condemnation of his contemporary society: "The social world is organized sin; . . . it is corruption even if outwardly and in appearance it announces its intention to do good." Quoted by Msgr. Debout. On several occasions he warned the priests of St. Francis de Sales against Catholic liberalism, which seemed to him to be disobedience to the pope.

[294] This is evident in Fr. Chaumont's defence of the Communard officer arrested "with his arms in hand"—the opposite of his convictions. But the priest pleaded successfully for him before a military tribunal.

director, Fr. Chaumont followed the women he directed patiently and over the long term, always aware that progress toward living the way of the Gospels can be slow. In this ministry he was "all things to all," completely available to those who sought him. He knew that he had to let go of his own personality, never allowing himself to force his will on someone who came to him for spiritual guidance. He had to allow himself to be the channel for the Holy Spirit, so that Jesus himself, through the medium of his words, would be the guide for their souls. A spiritual director should not try to attach those he counsels to himself, but seek only their spiritual progress and salvation. He himself was absolutely obedient to his own spiritual director, Msgr. de Ségur, then later Fr. Tissot, welcoming their advice as if it came from the Divine Will.

Speaking to the Priests of St. Francis de Sales, he adopted the same tone of voice: he did not promise them an earthly reward: having souls "in their care" requires great self-sacrifice and often brings suffering. He spoke in a similar way to his Daughters, inviting them to feel the deepest compassion for those they would be guiding: *"It is impossible to guide souls without being bound closely to their fate."* [295] His personal spirituality followed such an attitude of compassion to the point that it might be called

---

[295] Even though he prescribed some acts of mortification and renunciation for some of the women under his spiritual guidance, he knew that it was difficult to maintain a balance between the demands of a Christian life and those of a certain social class, especially for married women.

"doloriste" [exultation of suffering].[296] If such practices are not easily understood in our times, we should remember that it was the transposition into corporal terms of the deep, fraternal sympathy he felt for the suffering of the people he met.

Henri Chaumont was always demanding of his own strength, refusing to give in to his own pain, allowing himself few pleasures, and always "reasonable" ones.[297] Even near the end of his life, already partly disabled by his bad health, he continued to visit the residents of his area of Paris and continued to serve those who needed his ministry.

Once again following the teachings of Msgr. de Ségur, he set himself apart from anything resembling Gallicanism or Jansenism, encouraging frequent communion and *ultramontaine** devotions, such as devotion to the Sacred Heart. It was the "blind prelate" who led him to great closeness to Jesus, constantly present in his writings and his words. He had the figure of God as judge always before him, but always

---

[296] It seems that suffering was even sought out as a means of expiation, not only for himself but also for the souls he guided.

[297] Nevertheless, he learned from St. Francis de Sales that he should maintain a spirit of joy and good humor, rather than a cold severity that might cause discouragement in his followers. This was how he lived in community with several priests of St. Francis de Sales toward the end of his life. His moderation was evident but his guests moderated what could have become too much rigor. The use of reason in structuring one's life is a Salesian heritage. He refused all useless luxury, remaining faithful to the code of the "White Oak Society," which went back to his years in the seminary.

tempered by the thought of the gentle Jesus, which brought warmth to his austere spirituality and led him to peace in his soul. Thus he was able to escape from the "sickness of scrupulosity" that had disturbed him during a period of his adolescence. The Holy Spirit is first of all "the Spirit of Jesus,"[298] seen as a guide in the life of priests and in the life of all Christians. He saw it also as the principle of all supernatural love, "making all souls holy."

Fr. Chaumont never stopped repeating that to learn from the school of St. Francis de Sales is not to adopt a particular spirituality touching just one aspect of life, but to learn directly from Jesus, imitating him in all ways and working for one's perfection:

We do not lose our courage, even though the outer man may perish, our inner being is every day renewed, because the affliction of the present moment produces glory beyond measure, our eyes are not fixed on visible things but on the invisible, for the visible lasts only for a little time; the invisible is eternal. (2 Cor 4:16–18.)

---

[298] The Society of Priests of St. Francis de Sales was originally known as the Society of Priests of the Spirit of Jesus.
*Editor's note: Devotions approved by the Vatican; see footnote #72.

Prayer for the Beatification of Henri Chaumont:

Oh God, you call your disciples to holiness through different states of life and you inspired Fr. Chaumont, your servant, to guide them to accomplish your will by living the evangelical counsels, in the spirit of St. Francis de Sales. Listen to our prayer and deign to glorify him who has worked tirelessly to establish your kingdom. We ask this prayer through Christ our Lord. Amen.

Prayer for the Beatification of the Venerable Caroline Carré de Malberg:

Lord, you put in the heart of Caroline Carré the desire to love you without refusing you anything. Following her example, make me live by the Spirit of Jesus, welcoming daily events according to God's plan.

Deign to manifest her holiness in granting, through her intercession, the graces necessary for me, through Jesus Christ our Lord. Amen.

Prayer for the Beatification of the Servant of God Marie Gertrude Gross:

God, our Father, we praise and thank you for the gift of your servant, Mother Marie Gertrude, who sought your will in everything.

You blessed her with a passionate love for Jesus, a total confidence in Mary Immaculate and a deep life of prayer.

With an ardent zeal for mission, as a living gospel, she spent her life at the service of women and the poor.

Through her intercession grant us the grace we ask you now . . . , deign to manifest her holiness and count her among your saints. We make this prayer through Christ our Lord. Amen.

CONTACTS

French website : **francoisdesales.com**
Association Saint François de Sales
57-59 rue Léon Frot
75011 Paris, FRANCE
Tel: 33-01-43-67-60-60
e-mail: centresa@free.fr

U.S.A. website: **www.sfdsassociation.org**

Salésiennes Missionnaires de Marie Immaculée
(Salesian Missionaries of Mary Immaculate)
17 Villa Rémond
94250 Gentilly, FRANCE
Tel: 33-01-49-12-03-80
e-mail: generalatsmmi.gentilly@orange.fr

Priests of Saint Francis de Sales
22 rue de Varenne
Tel: 33-01-45-48-56-50
75007 Paris, FRANCE
e-mail: pfsf@wanadoo.fr

Sons of Saint Francis de Sales
Same address as Priests of Saint Francis de Sales
e-mail: filsfs@yahoo.fr

BIBLIOGRAPHY

[Abbé BARTHELEMY], *Saint Marcel, évêque et patron de Paris. Son culte, le quartier, la paroisse*, Paris, Téqui, 1914, 143p.

Jacques-Olivier BOUDON, *Paris capitale religieuse sous le Second Empire*, (Histoire religieuse de la France, 18), Paris, Le Cerf, 2001, 560p.

Henri CHAUMONT, *La Première Mère de la Société des Filles de Saint-François de Sales*, Paris, Au siège de la Société, 1894, XIV-595p.

Robert de COURCEL, *La Basilique de Sainte Clotilde*, impr. Lescuyer, Lyon, 1957, 226p.

Mgr Henri DEBOUT, *Le Chanoine Henri Chaumont et la sanctification du prêtre*, Paris, La Bonne Presse, 1930, VIII-364p.

Marthe de HÉDOUVILLE, *Monseigneur de Ségur. Sa vie – son action (1820-1881)*, Paris, Nouvelles Éditions latines, 1957, 701p.

Mgr LAVEILLE, *Madame Carré de Malberg, fondatrice de la Société des Filles de Saint François de Sales (1829-1891) d'après des documents inédits*, Tours, Mame – Paris, Téqui, 1917, XX-513p.Id.,

L'Abbé Henri Chaumont, Tours, Mame – Paris, Téqui, 1919, XXII-580p.

Découvrir Henri Chaumont et sa famille spirituelle, Marseille, Impr. ECE, 1996, 45p.

Diocèse de Paris. Procès de l'Ordinaire de M. Chaumont, ms., 5 vol., 1482+272+38p.

Henri Chaumont et la sanctification des laïcs, préface de Mgr Maziers, archevêque de Bordeaux, Paris, centre salésien, sd, Impr. Administrative centrale, 63p.

[*Summarium*] *Parisien. Beatificationis et canonizationis servi Dei Henrici Chaumont sacerdotis et fundatoris societatis presbyterorum S. Francisci Salesii. Summarium super dubio an signanda sit commissio introductionis causae in casu et ad effectum de quo agitur*, s.l.s.d., 681p.

Fr. Chaumont in the garden of
rue de Bourgogne

Msgr de Ségur
1820 – 1881

French bishop and charitable pioneer. He was devoted to
St. Francis de Sales. In or around 1856, he became blind.
In 1881, he organized the first formal Eucharistic Congress
in Lille, France, attended by 4000 people.

The First 4 Catechist Missionaries of Mary Immaculate (CMMI) in France, the garden of rue de Bourgogne, before their departure for India.

L to R: Sr. Madeleine of the Bl. Sacrament, Mother Marie Gertrude, Mother Marie de Kostka and Sr. Joseph of the Visitation.

Mother Marie Gertrude and the first Catechist
Missionaries of Mary Immaculate with friends,
Nagpur, India, 1889

L to R: Sr. Madeleine, Mother Marie de Kostka, Mother
Marie Gertrude and Sr. Joseph, unknown mother and
children.

Made in the USA
Charleston, SC
11 November 2016